W9-ANN-532

ELECTRONIC JOB SEARCH REVOLUTION

WIN WITH THE NEW TECHNOLOGY THAT'S RESHAPING TODAY'S JOB MARKET

Joyce Lain Kennedy and Thomas J. Morrow

JOHN WILEY & SONS, INC.

New York ▪ Chichester ▪ Brisbane ▪ Toronto ▪ Singapore

Copyright © 1994 by Joyce Lain Kennedy and Thomas J. Morrow.
Published by John Wiley & Sons, Inc.

Library of Congress Cataloging in Publication Data:

Kennedy, Joyce Lain.
    Electronic job search revolution : win with the new technology
  that's reshaping today's job market / by Joyce Lain Kennedy and
  Thomas J. Morrow.
        p.   cm.
    Includes index.
    ISBN 0-471-59821-6 (cloth) — ISBN 0-471-59820-8 (pbk.)
    1. Job hunting—Technological innovations.   2. Job hunting—Data
  bases.   3. Help-wanted advertising—Data bases.   4. Employment
  services—Automation.   5. Resumes (Employment)—Data processing.
  I. Morrow, Thomas J.   II. Title.
  HF5382.7.K457   1994
  650.14—dc20   93-19665

Printed in the United States of America

10   9   8   7   6   5   4   3   2   1

For

Nondes Pitman Busby and **Lowrie Thatcher Busby**

> My favorite aunt and uncle
> Who kissed my life by making me
> the favorite niece.
>
> J.L.K.

Maurice E. Stamps

> My high school English teacher,
> football coach, and lifelong mentor,
> who taught me how to avoid
> committing homicide with
> The King's English.
>
> T.J.M.

Foreword

In today's organizations, the term "business as usual" has become obsolete, largely because of the role of technology.

More than ever before, technology has changed almost every facet of business. From telecommunications to robotics, technology has increased productivity and, in many cases, lowered the costs of doing business and the number of people necessary to perform certain functions.

This change hasn't occurred without a price. In recent years, many people have lost their jobs because of the recession and consequent restructuring at every level of almost every organization.

Besides the price paid in real terms by the people who have lost their jobs, the requirements for the remaining workers have increased as organizations have reduced staff while requiring the same work output as before. Organizations must try to get as much as they can out of the remaining employees through more effort, longer hours of work, and new technologies.

Technology has played a critical role in the contraction and restructuring of the work force, but, until recently, it had done little to assist people in their search for employment.

The necessity of a merger between new and evolving technology and human potential has become obvious.

In the job search, this need can be readily seen. The recruiting process was formerly somewhat analogous to a game of darts between novices: hit or miss. Now it is much closer to an art form, as tests and personality profiles give human resource (HR) professionals a better method to match the right persons to the right jobs, before they even meet the applicants.

New recruitment technology allows automatic elimination of candidates whose work experience and particular skill requirements do not fit the profiles for certain jobs, and offers more time to search for the remarkable candidate among a group of excellent candidates. This advantage serves both the human resource professional and the job applicant.

With the introduction of new technology in the workplace, the role of the human resource professional has developed and expanded. Not only must human resource professionals be proficient in the use of new technologies, but they need to know the best way to introduce them to employees, how to improve service, how to make sure that a new technology will not inhibit productivity, and how technology will reduce costs.

Thus, not only the role of technology will shape the work force, but the relationship of technology to the most important aspect of any business—the human component. Human resource professionals, therefore, are charged with merging new technology with human ability.

Past Meets Present

In the past, "personnel" departments benefited least from organizational funding and resources. The job of human resource professionals was to hire workers and to deal with employee problems. Now, the heads of human resource sections are key decision makers and leaders in those same organizations. Input from human resource departments is critical today in the planning and preparation of long- and short-term strategies, and HR knowledge, expertise, and training are invaluable to CEOs as they help map the future of organizations.

The impact of new technology in the workplace does not mean that former elements of the human resource profession are to be discarded. Even with electronic and voice mail systems, the importance of human contact remains extremely important to both customers and employees. Human resource professionals must give this new corporate structure a human face, not only in interviewing, but in explanations of benefits packages, problems in the workplace, safety and health concerns, and termination.

Even as the responsibilities and influence of HR professionals have grown in magnitude and importance, they have not been immune to the overhaul in corporate restructuring. In some cases, human resource departments have been sharply reduced in size, yet not in scope. With fewer people doing more work, technology has had to step in and fill the void. Less time can be spent by human resource professionals to find the right person for the right job. Old ways of resume collection and dissemination by staff are slow, tedious, and expensive.

Fortunately, technology has revolutionized the search for employment itself. A new and ever growing element of the technological age in the workplace can be found in recruitment databases, and there is little doubt that electronic recruitment will become a key component of employment searches—not only for the potential employee, but for employers as well.

More and more companies and their human resource departments are establishing automated applicant tracking systems and resume databases to assist in recruitment. With fewer resources and less time available to them, HR professionals are finding electronic recruitment invaluable.

Technology Meets Tradition

What does this revolution in the search for employment mean for the job seeker? Tried and true techniques of job hunting should not be discarded. Activities such as networking still remain a vital part of the job search. New technology is not foolproof, and letting people know—for instance, in your professional society—that you are searching for employment does and will continue to generate leads and potential results.

The interview still remains a crucial step in employment. However, the initial interviewer may be a computer that tests the prospective employee on his or her knowledge and disposition for solving problems. The results of the computer interview will be available to the second interviewer, a person.

Of all the new technology, resume databases and other forms of electronic searches hold the most in store for people searching for employment. They allow job seekers greater time for research on prospective employers, and opportunities to enter into direct contact with them. Applicants gain the ability to have their resumes read by potentially hundreds of employers for a fraction of the cost and time. The time and money saved can be better used by the job seeker. Thus, although new technology is a useful tool, it does not wipe away traditional methods of the job search—it augments them.

Electronic Job Search Revolution holds vital information about the resources available to merge new technology and the search for employment. This first-of-a-kind book is written in an easy-to-read, understandable style. Incorporated at every turn are suggestions from human resource specialists to help readers gain a better understanding of how to best use this valuable tool.

Joyce Lain Kennedy and Thomas J. Morrow have a wealth of knowledge and experience in bringing workplace issues and changes to the public, and this outstanding work is no exception. More and more information today is distributed and disseminated through computers and other electronic means, and at this important juncture where technology meets the job search of the 1990s, you will be in a position to benefit through their work.

Technology promises many positive developments for the modern job seeker and the human resource professional. Alone, technology is not enough; coupled with traditional methods of job hunting and recruiting, it can be a pillar of support and an outstanding ally.

MICHAEL R. LOSEY, SPHR, PRESIDENT
SOCIETY FOR HUMAN RESOURCE MANAGEMENT

Alexandria, Virginia

Michael R. Losey is a certified Senior Professional in Human Resources. He is president and chief executive officer of the Society for Human Resource Management, a professional membership organization representing more than 55,000 human resource professionals worldwide.

Trademarks

For readability, in this work vendor names are not set in capital letters, nor are the signs indicating trademarks or service marks used. All known marks are listed below. This list is not necessarily complete. Any use of marked names, whether on this list or not, is editorial and to the benefit of the mark holder. The marks appear below as they are used by the companies holding the marks.

Mark	Mark Holder
Abra Cadabra™	Abra Cadabra Software, Inc.
AbraScan™	Abra Cadabra Software, Inc.
AbraTrak™	Abra Cadabra Software, Inc.
ACCESS®	ACCESS Corporation
AM/2000™	SPECTRUM Human Resource Systems Corporation
America Online℠	America Online, Inc.
APN™	Academic Position Network
Business Dateline® Ondisc	UMI
Business ASAP™ on InfoTrac	Information Access Company
Business & Company ProFile™ on InfoTrac	Information Access Company
Career Link Worldwide™	Career Link Worldwide
Career Doctors BBS™	Career Doctors Bulletin Board Service
Career Navigator™	Drake Beam Morin, Inc.
Career Search™	Career Search
ClassiFACTS®	North American ClassiFACTS®, Inc.
CompuServe®	CompuServe Incorporated

Mark	Mark Holder
Computer Careers On-Line℠	C.W. Publishing, Inc.
Corporate Jobs Outlook!™	Corporate Jobs Outlook, Inc.
CorpTech®	Corporate Technology Information Services, Inc.
cors™	cors, Inc.
CrossWalk™	CrossWalk™
DescriptionsWrite Now!™	KnowledgePoint
DIALOG®	©DIALOG Information Services
Dovetail Software™	Dovetail Software™
Dow Jones News/Retrieval®	Dow Jones & Company, Inc.
DowQuest℠	Dow Jones & Company, Inc.
Duns Million Dollar Disc®	Dun & Bradstreet Information Services
EJM℠	Human Resource Management Center, Inc.
Electronic Job Matching℠	Human Resource Management Center, Inc.
Electronic Job Hunter™	On-Line Personnel Services
General BusinessFile™, Public Edition	Information Access Company
GEnie®	General Electric Network for Information Exchange
HUMAN RESOURCE INFORMATION CENTER™	Computing Management, Inc.
IBM PC®	International Business Machines Corporation
IBM®	International Business Machines Corporation
InfoTrac®	Information Access Company
IntelliView	Pinkerton Security and Investigation Services
Investext®	Thompson Financial Networks, Inc.
Job Bank USA™	Job Bank USA, Inc.
JOBTRAC®	JOBTRAC
JOBTRAK®	JOBTRAK
kiNEXUS℠	Information Kinetics, Inc.
LEXIS®/NEXIS®	Mead Data Central, Inc.
Macintosh®	Apple Computer, Inc.
Martindale-Hubbell®	Reed Reference Publishing Company
Moody's® Industrial Disc	Moody's Investors Services, Inc.
Moody's® Bank & Finance Disc	Moody's Investors Services, Inc.
National Resume Bank™	Professional Association of Resume Writers
On-Line Career Fair®	Response Technologies Corporation
PeopleSoft®	PeopleSoft, Inc.
PowerMatch®	Warren Wicke and Company
Prodigy®	Prodigy Services Company
RESTRAC™	MicroTrac Systems, Inc.

Mark	Mark Holder
RESUmate™	RESUmate, Inc.
Resumes-on-Computer™	Curtis Publishing Company
Resumix™	Resumix, Inc.
Sharkware™	CogniTech Corporation
SkillSearch™	SkillSearch Corporation
SmartSearch2™	Advanced Personnel Systems
SS2™	Advanced Personnel Systems
TCTN™	The Career Television Network™
The Interviewer®	Global Publishing Corp
Thomas Register of American Manufacturers®	Thomas Publishing Company
University ProNet℠	University ProNet, Inc.
Unix®	AT&T Bell Laboratories
WordPerfect®	WordPerfect Corporation

Acknowledgments

Our thanks to a great many people who have given us their valuable time, support, help, and encouragement, so that we might bring this book to reality. We thank you. And the job hunters of America thank you.

SPECIAL APPRECIATION

To **Muriel Wallace Turner,** for keeping us on track, on schedule, updated, and uplifted. You're the greatest!

EDITORIAL SUPPORT

Gayle Leslie Bryant, The Kennedy Office

ADVISERS

Jane Paradiso, Bell Atlantic Telephone
Sue Rugge, The Rugge Group
Peter Weddle, Job Bank USA
Mark Gisleson, Gisleson Writing Services
James M. Lemke, Resumix
David Geron, cors
Paul SerVas, Resumes-on-Computer
John Younger, Human Resource Professional
Pat Lindh, Public Relations Professional
Regina Aulisio, Marketing Professional
Robert L. Smith, Jr., Videotex Industry Association
Paula Davis, DORS, Defense Outplacement Referral System
      U.S. Department of Defense

RECRUITER

Eva M. June, Walling, June & Associates

PUBLISHING

At John Wiley & Sons: **Mike Hamilton, Fred Nachbaur, Elena Paperny, Karl Weber, Mary Daniello, Peter Clifton.** At Publications Development Company: **Maryan Malone, Nancy Marcus Land, Denise Netardus.**

Contents

Introduction

Whether you want a job this instant or have the foresight to be planning for your career advancement, *what you're about to read is really new!*

How many times have you picked up a book that promised to help you get a job—or to move up in life—only to realize you had already read the same ideas in other books? This isn't one of those. The following pages are neither retreads nor reruns of books you've already read about finding a job.

This book could not have been written earlier. The engines driving the job search revolution are only now coming together in our fast-moving, technology-escalated society.

The information we've gathered has never before been presented in a concise, comprehensive, here-it-is format. Bits and pieces have appeared in scattered media, but the trend-identifying big picture is presented here for the first time.

Before you can get the words "No way do I want to struggle through a technical book" out of your mouth, be assured that this book is an easy read.

You needn't be frightened or even apprehensive about what you're about to learn. We tell this complex story in a way that doesn't require knowing in advance any computerese. When we must use technical jargon, we explain what it means in everyday language. You don't have to be a technojock to understand and use profitably what you'll find here.

Remind yourself that you need not understand the inner workings of a clock to tell time, or know how to repair a car to drive one. To benefit from this book, it isn't necessary or even important that you understand anything about how a computer works.

In fact, we'll let you in on a secret. Both authors, Joyce and Tom, are dropouts from Techie U. Joyce keeps her copy of *WordPerfect for Dummies* as a desk reference. Tom says his learning curve on computers is somewhat slower than a speeding bullet. We're kidding, but only a little. The point is, both authors believe that if they were able to learn how job search technology works, anyone can learn it!

If you're an accomplished job hunter, *Electronic Job Search Revolution* along with its companion volume *Electronic Resume Revolution*, adds a fresh layer of expertise to your knowledge.

If you're a beginner—or haven't looked for a job in years—this book starts you off at the right place in time because it reflects the phenomenal shifts in the job market occurring, literally, as you read these words. (Yes, we *do* recommend that you beef up your overall job search skills by reading other job hunt guides.)

In these pages, we offer suggestions from human resource specialists working on the front lines—specialists who are using the incredible applicant tracking systems every day. We share interpretations from software authors. We reveal tips from database experts, many of whom are key movers in the job search revolution. This is what you'll learn, chapter-by-chapter:

▶ Chapter 1—an overview of how, in a job search, the computer has become as indispensable as film in a camera.

▶ Chapter 2—how independent database services register people and then permit employer clients to search for candidates who fit the jobs they're trying to fill.

▶ Chapter 3—how jobs are being filled with people whose resumes have been entered into the employer's own database.

▶ Chapter 4—companies and organizations that are operating on-line job databases, including help-wanted advertising.

▶ Chapter 5—the efficiencies of using employer databases to custom-design a list of job prospects. Databases are available on CD-ROM disks, computer disks, and online.

▶ Chapter 6—how the world of computerization has developed to the point where many companies allow computers to take initial applications from job seekers, and, in some cases, administer testing before the hiring process moves to the second level.

▶ Chapter 7—new technological innovations that both you and the human resource specialist can use. Most of the high-tech tools described here are with us today, and others are only a few years away. We predict that, before the 21st century arrives, job seekers will have frequent opportunities to present themselves on a CD-ROM disk or some similar video medium.

Electronic Job Search Revolution is a book of resources. It *has* to be, because there is no other way to document the dramatic recruitment innovations taking place across America.

We can shout "Job search is changing!" until we're blue in the face, but until you have the chance to see for yourself the myriad variations of the electronic job search universe, you may still be a doubter.

"You've got to make it believable—even if it's true," jokes Hershell Price, a San Diego friend of ours. After reading our manuscript, he says he is "astounded, just astounded!" Price adds that when the book is published, he wants to make sure that both of his adult daughters, facing the crowded labor market for new college graduates, get copies.

To save valuable time that you can better use for a job search, we have included dozens of company names, addresses, and telephone and fax numbers to use in your quest. We went to a lot of trouble to be certain the contact information is correct as we go to press. Let us hear from you (Kennedy and Morrow, P.O. Box 3090, Carlsbad, CA 92009) if you find errors or if company information changes. Things move speedily in the world of computerized resume databases and applicant tracking systems—and all the other wonders of innovation.

We didn't include every new project that came to our attention, either because some entrepreneurial efforts struck us as too visionary or because the newcomers were not scheduled to open their doors until after this book reached the bookstores.

Even with those ventures left out, the emerging electronic recruitment industry is vastly more widespread than we had imagined when we began researching this book.

In fact, we were planning to title Chapter 1 "It's Dawn Breaking Time on the New Job Market" because we thought we might be a little ahead of the curve. But after a year of deep digging into the topic, we realized the title should be "Dawn Has Broken on the New Job Market."

But these last words don't sound very exciting, and this is exciting stuff.

How do we open the book? Please turn the page.

1

"Sun Up" on the New Job Market

Hurry to Learn the New Tools and the New Rules of How You Look for a Job—It's the Change of the Century

This chapter identifies reasons why the job search revolution is racing across the concrete canyons and purple mountains and golden wheatfields of America. It explains why—at the beginning of this revolution—you should not prematurely toss out traditional job search methods but start now to add a new electronic edge to your job search skills.

For job seekers and rising stars alike, wonders may lie ahead. Change certainly does. In this decade that bridges the centuries, a quiet technological revolution, already begun, is reinventing the ways that people and jobs meet:

▶ Resumes zap across cities or countries by telephone lines.
▶ Help-wanted ads flash on home computer screens.
▶ Vast databases of resumes match people to jobs.
▶ Resumes are optically scanned, organized, stored, and pulled out in a wink.

▶ CD-ROMs and videos are used for interviewing.

▶ Electronic marvels make it easy to customize a blue-ribbon job hunt.

Paper is not out, but electronics are definitely in. Resourceful American job hunters who are looking for the big edge in a killer job market are finding something new in the air of America's corporate hiring halls: computer-driven job services.

Before you go into microchip shock, realize you need not have a technical aptitude to "go electronic." You need not even *like* computers to feel the earth move in the emerging upheaval. But the earth is moving: Computerized job services and the electronic recruitment industry are taking over where traditional paper methods leave off.

As technology sparks new ways to look for a job and new ways to find people to hire, the job search revolution has indeed begun.

What forces are spanking new life into a job search revolution at this particular moment in our history? In the ways we look for work, what are the engines driving the biggest employment matchmaking change in a century? Briefly, here's the explanation.

The great job express that rolled through the decades since World War II has run out of gas. As the late Dan Lacey, editor of the newsletter *Workplace Trends*, observed:

"Our country and our culture have not yet grasped what is going on. . . . We are at the end of the post-World War II boom days. Everything that everyone considers normal about work—long-term steady employment with a full range of company-paid benefits and ever rising wages—is a way of life that came about in America after World War II. It never existed anywhere else."

In the 1980s, American employers, desperate to stay competitive, cut millions of people from their payrolls. The cuts included human resource specialists, who had been the grand gatekeepers for corporate America. The carnage produced a historically significant trend: the steady and permanent elimination of millions of jobs. Those jobs won't be coming back.

An avalanche of company cutbacks introduced a new word in our culture—the dreaded "downsizings." Huge numbers of experienced, qualified workers were thrown into a frenzied competition for jobs. Now, fearful of being overwhelmed with applicants, employers are thinking twice about advertising job openings.

Each time a job opening for a good position hits print, companies are set upon by hoards of job seekers. Because corporate chieftains have thinned the ranks of the human resource departments in the downsizings, they have sometimes left themselves woefully short of staff to respond to hundreds of applications for each job opening. Many companies simply don't have enough people to react in the old-fashioned way—sorting people by hand.

In one instance, a major employer in the Midwest received 10,000 resumes in a one-month period. The human resource staff tried valiantly to cope with skyscrapers of paper by holding "resume parties." At these "parties," a dozen or so people worked in a conference room late into many nights, eating sandwiches and sorting resumes. They saw more of the resumes than they did of their families.

"After finding, say, 172 good candidates for a position, we stopped sorting through—even though we knew the very best candidate may well have been number 173 or 178," says a survivor of the ordeal. "It was exhausting to keep reading resumes after a certain point. And the more resumes we read, the less time we had to interview. It was a Catch-22."

Moving beyond the technical problem of too many applicants and too few people to screen them, observers generally agree that, philosophically, the United States has become a bottom-line economy. These are the new rules:

▶ Profit or perish.
▶ Push for high performance figures for the annual report.
▶ Get more sales, more revenues.
▶ Keep the stockholders happy: Keep the company in the black.
▶ Stay alive: Think *money, money, money!*

In our bottom-line economy, employers are in a take-no-prisoners revolt against hiring costs that have risen like college tuitions. They are constantly on the lookout for ways to trim a budget line and nip an inflated figure.

The trauma and turmoil in the employment arena will continue. Saving on expenses has become a way of life as the nation's businesses fight off global competition, restructure to survive the end of the World War II boom years, and salt away money to buy technologically advanced equipment to stay in business.

The cost per hire for professional and managerial personnel averages $5,400, says a recent study by the Employment Management Association, an organization of employment and personnel executives in business, education, and industry. When a private recruitment firm is used, the average cost per hire rockets to $35,300.

At a time when employers are trying to send hiring costs downward, another trend is moving up on the charts: the proliferation of computers in homes, where most job search planning takes place.

Human Resource Automation Helps One of Its Own

Adina Marcheschi of Chicago is a human resource specialist who knows more than she ever wanted to about the term "downsizing."

After losing her job, she began networking and answering help-wanted ads. The competition was frightful. Marcheschi says employers told her she was competing with 300 resumes.

A member of the Society for Human Resource Management, Marcheschi took advantage of a benefit available to society members, a free one-year membership in Job Bank USA, a McLean, Virginia, independent resume database firm that surfaces candidates for job openings.

A few months later, Marcheschi was offered and accepted a position as the corporate recruiter for the National Easter Seal Society.

Now, as a recruiter, she understands electronic employment matchmaking from both sides of the desk.

One out of every four households has a home computer, according to Link Resources, a market research firm in New York. By mid-decade, Link expects that figure to rise to more than one out of every three.

The numbers encourage us to agree with Victor Hugo's often quoted comment: "An invasion of armies can be resisted, but not an idea whose time has come."

Computers are here. People no longer use them as expensive paperweights. People are no longer afraid of them. People who are not the technically elite are seeing computers as one of life's requirements.

Equally important, companies no longer can support the hand-sorting of people that has taken place during the entire 20th century. Manual personnel systems are under intense scrutiny. Their cost-effectiveness is daily questioned by managers for whom the bottom line is sacred.

A marriage of two trends is fueling the job search revolution: unyielding pressure on business to cut costs while dealing with armies of job seekers, and the new wave of user-friendly technology. The result is an explosion of new tools and new rules that is changing forever how you should look for work.

Presenting yourself using old guidelines we've all learned and become familiar with over the years could now hurt your chances of landing your dream job.

HOW TO KEEP YOUR HEAD IN THE REVOLUTION

During all of this century, job seekers have found employment in familiar ways. They have studied the newspaper help-wanted ads, made inquiries at company personnel offices, signed up with employment services, sent out resumes and asked around in what came to be known as "making contacts" or "networking."

Although no single aspect of this ritualistic pursuit has been eliminated, everything you thought you knew about job hunting is no longer enough to keep you out of the rain in a downpour of joblessness.

Are we saying that the advice you're absorbing from job search books and from job coaches is obsolete? Not at all. Some verities really are eternal, and we advise you to heed the abiding truths shared by authors and counselors you admire. What we recommend is that

---

The New Job Search Rulebook

You can't count on getting today's jobs with yesterday's search techniques.

Become aware of the digital age as it affects job search.

Anyone who is thinking about the future will have to self-market around the clock.

Educate yourself about being visible in databases 24 hours a day, 7 days a week.

During this time of technology transition, plan on doing a two-tier job search: one for humans, one for computers.

Learn how computers differ from humans in how they read resumes and screen applicants.

You'll create your own job security by developing computer search skills.

From picking through employer databases to online searching, computers have become a friendly way to find jobs.

Never assume the way you've always job hunted is a sure thing.

Consider job search a matter of continuing education requiring lifelong attention.

---

you add a new layer of contemporary information to the knowledge you already have about effective ways to job hunt.

A childhood couplet makes the point vividly:

> Make new friends and keep the old,
> One is silver, the other gold.

Job hunting isn't what it used to be. It's time to toss out some of the old nuggets that just won't work for you anymore.

This book and its companion guide, *The Resume Revolution*, introduce you to new technologies that may astound you. Most are in use already and some are nearly here.

As a popular computer command says, GO. On with the revolution!

2

Independent Resume Database Services

Robot Recruiters That Can Do Wonders for Your Career—Or Then Again, Your Name May Never Come Up

This chapter focuses on external, third-party resume database services—independent firms that register people in their databases and then permit employers to draw from the databases when searching for people to hire.

Some databases are open to all comers, and you can get your resume included free or by paying a fee. Entry to other databases hinges on your level of experience (new graduate or seasoned worker), your occupation, or your membership in a professional association.

Quick—what's the best thing that can happen to your job search? It's over and you've won the job you want! Okay, okay, the second best.

If you say you'd like to have a recruiter working for you 24 hours a day, 7 days a week, matching—in minutes or even in seconds—your qualifications with open job requisitions, you may get your wish.

The recruiters that make this magic in blanketing the job market with your qualifications are computerized services. They're called electronic resume databases.

Independent electronic resume database services are springing up across the nation as increasing numbers of people discover and use this innovative and relatively inexpensive job recruitment channel.

Database users fall in three main groups:

1. Individuals who hope to find employment quickly by listing their resumes in databases.

2. Individuals who do not necessarily hope to find employment quickly by listing their resumes in databases, but who understand the vital importance of visibility in career management. They're "on display" when employers go shopping for personnel.

3. Employers who search databases to find people to fill open positions. Client employers can use these computerized recruiters with the ease of a few strokes on a computer keyboard or a telephone call any hour of the day and night. The search can be launched from virtually any point on the globe.

Individuals can access the resume databases at will. No gatekeeping secretaries are on duty to prevent you from contacting the recruiter you hope to attract.

If the concept of electronic recruiting tools is unfamiliar, let's start with a basic question: What is a resume database?

The short answer is that it's a collection of individual resumes stored in a computer. More precisely, a resume database service:

▶ Classifies
▶ Codes
▶ Stores   a group of resumes that have been
▶ Retrieves   entered into the system.
▶ Transmits

(A databank is a collection of databases, but the terms are often used interchangeably.)

Most resume databases are registries of people looking for a job, rather than inventories of job openings. But some services are in the business of listing job openings as well as registering individual applicants.

Each resume database service has a different way of doing business. In some systems, a computer extracts data from a resume or a

---

How Employers Hear about You

Resume database services may provide employer clients with information in one or more of six basic modes:

1. Summary, followed by ORIGINAL RESUME at a later time.
2. Summary, followed by STANDARDIZED PROFILE at a later time.
3. Summary with ORIGINAL RESUME at the same time.
4. Summary with STANDARDIZED PROFILE at the same time.
5. ORIGINAL RESUME only (paper or e-mail).
6. STANDARDIZED PROFILE only (paper or e-mail).

If you are a new graduate or have "hard" skills to offer, it may not matter whether you are marketed by an image of your original resume or by a standardized profile.

But, if you have "soft" skills and experience, an image of your original resume may be more effective than a standardized profile, because you have more opportunity to individualize your presentation.

---

standardized profile form. Then the computer sorts the information into categories such as position sought, industry, work history, occupational skills, education, salary expectation, years of experience, geographic locations preferred, ethnicity (a voluntary option), and willingness to relocate.

The information may be scanned in automatically and stored in the original resume format or in a standardized profile format. Most often, a crisp summary for each individual is computer-created.

In other systems, an employee of the service, rather than a computer system, abstracts relevant information and keywords to compose mini-profiles (summaries) and standardized profile forms.

Client employers can choose to receive any of the above combinations, view the data electronically, or receive paper printouts of resumes or standardized profile forms.

Figure 2–1 is a standardized form used by Access, a service discussed later in this chapter, for individuals seeking jobs in the accounting field. Employers receive both the filled-out form and a resume for each candidate who closely matches the requested search criteria.

A Career Placement Registry standardized form for experienced personnel is shown in Figure 2–2. After the form is filled out, the information is sent to an online service where employers can see it. Figure 2–2 shows only a portion of the form.

Return completed form to ACCESS Corporation, 1900 W. 47th Place, Ste. 215, Shawnee Mission, KS 66205-1801.
RETURN OF THIS FORM IS REQUIRED BEFORE INCLUSION IN SEARCHES.

Name _____   Telephone Number_____

PROFILE FORM - ACCOUNTING

Minimum Salary Desired _ _ , _ _ _ (Do not leave blank) Are you open to relocation (Yes or No)? _____
Are there any areas of Metropolitan K.C. where you do not want to work?_____
Type of work sought _____ (F)ull, (P)art-Time, or (T)emporary - Combine letters if more than one.

List 3 occupations for which you would like to be considered (i.e. Payroll Clerk, Controller): (SEE BACK)
1. _____ 2. _____ 3. _____
Number of years of overall work experience: _____ years. Number of companies worked for in last 5 years ____

Are you authorized to work full-time in the U.S.? ____ (Yes or No) Please circle (optional):   Male or Female
Indicate race or ethnic origin (optional) _____ (White Caucasian, African American, Hispanic, or Other)
If other, be specific _____

Education Level	High School	Undergraduate College/University	Graduate/ Professional
School Name/City & State:			
Years Completed (Circle):	9 10 11 12	1 2 3 4	1 2 3 4
Diploma/Degree:			
Course of Study:			

Have you had direct management or supervisory experience (Yes or No)? ___
If yes, how many are/were you directly responsible for? ____

Please answer only those questions that are applicable:
CPA (Yes or No) ____   Big 6 firm experience (Yes or No) ____
Years of public accounting experience: Audit ____, Tax ____, Consulting ____
Years of private industry experience: Financial ____, Treasury ____, Internal Audit ____, Other ____
List accounting functions performed _____.
(such as GL, AR, AP, Payroll, Inventory Control, Fixed Assets, Cost Accounting, Manufacturing, Bookkeeping)

Proficiency with these software programs _____.
    (Be prepared for testing--Proficiency implies full understanding)
Types of computer systems used on regular basis _____.

Years of data entry experience _____   Years of 10-key experience _____

Why are you motivated to look for a new job?_____
_____
_____.

** Do you want your search confidential? ____ (Yes or No). If yes, please indicate those companies you do not want
to receive your resume or profile information: _____
_____.

Figure 2–1   A Sample Database Standardized Profile Form

CAREER PLACEMENT REGISTRY — EXPERIENCED DATA ENTRY FORM

Please type or print in dark ink. Please complete sections B through F as fully as possible. Do not alter the form, improvise, or extend information beyond the space provided. Remember to sign the back of the form. Return completed form and check or money order for the amount indicated by the Fee Schedule shown on the back of this form to:

Career Placement Registry, 3202 Kirkwood Highway, Wilmington, Delaware 19808

A	Office Use Only

Copyright © 1986
Career Placement Registry, Inc.
302 Swann Avenue
Alexandria, Virginia 22301
(800) 368-3093
IN VIRGINIA (703) 683-1085

A01 _____
CPR Registration Number

A03 _____   A04 Country
Organization No.   Code

A02 Control Code
☐ 0 ☐ 1 ☐ 2 ☐ 3
☐ 4 ☐ 5 ☐ 6 ☐ 7
☐ 8 ☐ 9 ☐ A ☐ B
☐ C ☐ D ☐ E ☐ X

B	Personal Information

B01 _____
Last name of registrant

B02 _____
First name and middle initial

B03 Date available
for employment   Month — Year

B08 _____
Permanent address: Street

B09 _____
City

B10 _____ State

B11 _____ Zip Code

B13 Home Telephone Number ___-___-___
(Include Area Code)

B14 Work Telephone Number ___-___-___
(Include Area Code)

B15 Citizenship Status
☐ 1 — U. S. Citizen
☐ 2 — Permanent Visa
☐ 3 — Temporary Visa
☐ 4 — Student Visa
☐ 5 — Other

B16 Security Clearance
☐ 1 — Yes   ☐ 2 — No

C	Career Objectives

C01 Occupational Preferences. You may indicate up to three preferences.

☐ 01 — Accounting
☐ 02 — Administration
☐ 03 — Advertising
☐ 04 — Agriculture
☐ 05 — Animal Sciences
☐ 06 — Architecture
☐ 07 — Aviation/Aerospace
☐ 08 — Biological/Life Sciences
☐ 09 — Business
☐ 10 — Communications
☐ 11 — Computer Science
☐ 12 — Construction
☐ 13 — Criminology

☐ 14 — Data Processing
☐ 15 — Earth Sciences
☐ 16 — Economics
☐ 17 — Education/Training
☐ 18 — Electronics
☐ 19 — Engineering
☐ 20 — Finance
☐ 21 — Food Services
☐ 22 — Government
☐ 23 — Health Services
☐ 24 — Human Resources
☐ 25 — Human Services
☐ 26 — Information Science

☐ 27 — Insurance
☐ 28 — Journalism
☐ 29 — Labor Relations
☐ 30 — Legal Services
☐ 31 — Linguistics
☐ 32 — Management
☐ 33 — Manufacturing
☐ 34 — Marketing
☐ 35 — Medical Services
☐ 36 — Maintenance/Repair
☐ 37 — Performing Arts
☐ 38 — Physical Sciences
☐ 39 — Product Management

☐ 40 — Public Relations
☐ 41 — Publishing
☐ 42 — Purchasing
☐ 43 — Real Estate
☐ 44 — Recreation
☐ 45 — Retailing
☐ 46 — Sales
☐ 47 — Secretarial
☐ 48 — Social Sciences
☐ 49 — Technician
☐ 50 — Tourism
☐ 51 — Transportation
☐ 52 — Visual Arts

C02 _____
Type of position desired. (Be specific, do not abbreviate)

C03 Overall Work Experience
☐ 1 — (1–3 years) ☐ 2 — (4–6 years) ☐ 3 — (7–10 years) ☐ 4 — (11 or more years)

C04 Willingness to Travel
☐ 1 — (None) ☐ 2 — (25%) ☐ 3 — (50%) ☐ 4 — (75%) ☐ 5 — (100%)

C05 Willing to Relocate?
☐ — Yes   ☐ — No

C06 Expected Salary Range in thousands, please check at least one:
☐ 10 – 20 ☐ 30 – 40 ☐ 50 – 60 ☐ 70 – 80 ☐ 90 – 99 ☐ OPEN
☐ 20 – 30 ☐ 40 – 50 ☐ 60 – 70 ☐ 80 – 90 ☐ 100 or more

C07 Minimum Annual Salary Expected $_____

C08 Geographic Location Preference(s); please check at least one.

☐ 01 — Nationwide
(Anywhere in U.S.)

☐ 02 — Northeast
(CT, MA, ME, NH, RI, VT)

☐ 03 — Southeast
(AL, FL, GA, MS, SC)

☐ 04 — Middle Atlantic
(DC, DE, MD, NJ, NY, PA)

☐ 05 — Middle South
(KY, NC, TN, VA, WV)

☐ 06 — North Central
(IA, KS, MN, MO, NE, ND, SD)

☐ 07 — South Central
(AR, LA, OK, TX)

☐ 08 — Middle West
(IL, IN, MI, OH, WI)

☐ 09 — Northwest
(AK, ID, OR, WA)

☐ 10 — Southwest
(AZ, CA, HI, NV)

☐ 11 — Rocky Mountain
(CO, MT, NM, UT, WY)

☐ 12 — International
(Anywhere outside U.S.)

C09 _____
City preference(s) if applicable

C10 _____
Geographic Objections

Figure 2–2   A Sample Database Registration Form

Figure 2–3 represents two pages (actual documents may be longer) of the standard resume SkillSearch sends to employers. It is formatted by an automated process within the database and does not vary.

As an independent job seeker, you can access the resume database services in two basic ways:

1. *Mail, fax, or hand-deliver your resume to a resume database service.* A summary may be keyboarded into the database by an employee, or a summary and the entire resume may be inserted electronically using a scanner and OCR (optical character recognition) software. (Caution: Faxes or even some dot-matrix-printed materials often don't scan very well. People don't always read them too well, either.)

2. *Use a modem-equipped computer to transmit your resume electronically.* For those not yet literate in computerese, a modem is an inexpensive device that permits information to be transferred from one computer to another via telephone lines or radio waves. A fax/modem is ideal for moving resumes electronically. It works like a fax machine but places information, not a paper message, into the receiving computer.

As mentioned earlier, some services ask for a paper resume, and others require you to fill in the blanks of a standardized profile form. Some request both. In discussing specific database services later in this chapter, we distinguish between these two formats. You may feel that one or the other best showcases your qualifications.

Concepts are another matter; for simplicity in talking about marketing yourself in ways that may be unfamiliar, *we refer to both the paper resume and the standardized profile form as "resumes."*

WHAT RESUME DATABASE SERVICES OFFER YOU

What are the benefits of using electronic clearinghouses that can match job seekers with job openings at the touch of a computer key? We group them into the following main categories.

Access

Have you had this experience? You mail your resume to hordes of employers. You're sure that they *must* have need for the kind of work

David A. Sampleperson
102 Woodmont Blvd.
Nashville, TN 37205
(615) 383-4700

SELECTED ACHIEVEMENTS

- *Earned 5 consecutive 100% club awards. Quota was increased by 20% each year.*
- *22% revenue growth year-to-year, resulting in over $6,500,000 gross last year.*
- *Ranked in top 3% of entire field marketing force.*

EXPERIENCE

1987
to
Present

National Business Machines Corp.
Nashville, TN

Advisory Marketing Representative

Key responsibilities include marketing all NBM products and services
to customers in my assigned territory. Responsible for all customer
satisfaction, account coverage needs, maintaining customer executive
contacts, and quota attainment. Achieved 115% of assigned quota in
1990 and earned fifth consecutive 100% club award. In 1990 gained
100% customer satisfaction on accounts surveyed and increased
revenues by $1,200,000, which represents a 22% increase over 1989.
Total revenues for 1990 totaled over $6,500,000.

1986
to
1987

National Business Machines Corp.
Nashville, TN

Marketing Representative

Responsible for new accounts and first-time users of small to mid-range
computer systems. Covered a broad geographic territory in middle
Tennessee. Sold and installed over 40 new accounts in 1987 which was
the highest total for the Nashville office in that year. Earned the
"Golden Circle Award" and 100% club. Only top 3% of all reps
qualify for the Golden Circle each year.

Figure 2-3   Sample Database Resume

David A. Sampleperson
Page 2

1985
to
1986

National Business Machines Corp.
Atlanta, GA

Associate Marketing Representative

Key objectives were to complete training and gain thorough understanding of the entire product line. Finished in the top 10% of class and was elected President of Sales School Class.

EDUCATION

B.B.A., Duke University, 6/84
Major: Business Administration and Management
Major: Marketing
Minor: Computer Science
Dean's List 1983, Finished in Top 9% of Graduating Class

PROFESSIONAL ASSOCIATIONS

President, Young Executive's Club 1990
Member, Chamber of Commerce
Member, Marketing Management Association

COMMUNITY ACTIVITIES

Board of Directors, Grassland Middle School
Committee Member, United Way of Tennessee

SALES EXPERIENCE

Telemarketing, 1.0 yrs
Forecasting, 5.0 yrs
Cold Calling, 3.0 yrs
Market Research, 2.0 yrs
One on One Presentations, 5.0 yrs
Financial Justifications, 5.0 yrs
Group Presentations, 3.0 yrs
Executive Marketing, 3.0 yrs
Technical Sales, 5.0 yrs

Figure 2–3 *Continued*

you can do superbly. And you never hear back—or, if you do get a response, it's a form letter rejection ("Thank you for your interest in our company, but . . .").

Your target companies may be drowning in resumes. They just can't get around to seriously looking at yours. It isn't unusual for big corporations to receive hundreds of thousands of unsolicited resumes each year. Even midsize companies often are submerged in a torrent of thousands of resumes, and smaller firms may be underwater with hundreds of them.

When you have what an employer wants, using an electronic clearinghouse makes it more likely that your resume will "rise to the top of the stack" and be noticed. You can get immediate, comprehensive exposure.

Computerized resumes can be accessed and sorted in a number of ways. In a database of 1 million resumes, sorting by occupation, specialty skills, and location preference used to take up to 20 minutes or more to complete; now it takes only seconds.

As one database operator comments, "If a company wants to hire a violinist who speaks Portuguese and wishes to work in Omaha, we can locate that person—if he or she exists—in five seconds."

Wider Access

Perhaps the biggest advantage of going online with your resume is sheer numbers. You have the opportunity of putting your qualifications before an enormous number of organizations anywhere in the world—many more than you may be able to place on your own.

Speed

Electronic resume databases can be accessed by client companies quickly. Your background and qualifications become instantly available to employment recruiters.

Cost

Preparing and reproducing quality resumes can quickly eat up hundreds of dollars in reproduction expenses, supplies, and postage. Listing your resume in a database is relatively inexpensive—less than $100 in most cases. It may even be free, depending on the service you select. The free database listings are supported by large organizations that use the services to recruit new hires.

Confidentiality

Most of the services do not allow employers to browse through the resumes they have on file. Instead, employers tell the service what kind of job they want to fill and what qualifications they are expecting from the prospective employee. A database service employee then searches the database.

Applicants usually are listed by a code number rather than by name. Even so, because job seekers usually list their former employers by name and describe their previous positions, it wouldn't take a rocket scientist to find out who's who in a "village" industry, where everyone knows everyone. A current employer who is familiar with an employee's work history is likely to recognize a job-seeking employee from his or her resume.

Your only guarantee of confidentiality is the word of the service that your present employer—or any other party you specify—will not see your resume. Has the system ever broken down, revealing a job seeker's name to his or her own boss? Yes, one service owner candidly admits. But it was a fluke, he insists, happening only once in three years of operation.

Having issued this warning, we can give you happier news: In the vast majority of cases, it's highly unlikely that your cover will be blown.

Most services do not sell their names for use as mailing lists. Nevertheless, it's prudent to ask. Never assume anything.

Career Management

Database insertions permit currently employed individuals to gain wide exposure to many employers because, in effect, applications can be made after normal working hours. Being listed in one or more appropriate databases is good career insurance. It can become a permanent career-enhancement tool, identifying professional, managerial, and executive opportunities throughout one's career. As part of a positive approach to career management, being database proactive is like being on the right corner at the right time when the right bus comes along.

Who can find out about you—that is, *who knows you*—is just as important to career success as *whom you know*.

An example of the importance of visibility is Tim Harrel (not his real name), a software engineer in Colorado. Harrel was in a commercial resume database for a year and received only two taps on the shoulder. One was of no interest but the second was enticing enough to lure him to Boston. "I would never have known about my excellent current position if they hadn't spotted me in that database," he says.

Fairness

In theory, resume databases allow job seekers to be judged solely on qualifications such as experience, education, and skills.

A recruiter, for example, can tell the system to locate only those candidates who have a specific number of years on a particular type of job, who have worked for specific companies, who have graduated from specific universities, who have particular job skills, and who know specified programming languages.

In the normal course of events, the computer will not weed out female from male candidates or discriminate against applicants from diverse backgrounds or those with disabilities. Reality suggests it probably is too soon to know exactly how the claimed advantage of fairness will materialize.

WHAT RESUME DATABASE SERVICES DO NOT OFFER YOU

Although the rules of job shopping are changing, some things remain beyond the electronic reach. A resume database service usually does *not* offer you the following features.

Personal Representation

As a rule, resume database firms find people for jobs, not jobs for people. Most services are not designed to act as private employment agents.

We hasten to add that there are exceptions, and that there will be more as the industry matures. We describe in this chapter three services that do try to find jobs for people. Two services (Career Database and National Resume Bank) are funded entirely by applicant-paid fees. The other (cors) charges an additional but moderate fee if the job seeker wishes the service to match a resume with recruitment ads in major newspapers as well as openings in the service's client base.

Chance to Relax

Just because a resume database theoretically can produce results quickly doesn't mean you can kick back and ignore traditional ways to job hunt. Don't forget about networking, direct application, recruitment ads, and employment services.

If you really want to find a good job, work at your job hunt 40 to 80 hours a week and cover all the bases. This effort, added to your new electronic job search savvy, will put you way ahead of 99 percent of your competitors.

LOSERS AND WINNERS

Unfortunately, job seekers who need employment right this minute may not get offers on that schedule because this method does not tap into the "hidden job market"—unadvertised jobs, in the classic use of the term.

Employers may not even know they need to fill some of these jobs; if they do realize it, they haven't gotten around to the task.

In a computerized job search, you can't persuade employers to create a job or to fill an opening now instead of later. If an employer does not list a job vacancy or search for a candidate to fill it, the match won't be made.

Another aspect of electronic recruitment somewhat modifies that statement. In an employment market where there are many more applicants than jobs, a number of employers are beginning to use resume databases as their initial recruiting effort, to see whether they can fill vacant jobs without the expense of advertising or hiring employment services. By being in a database, you may be able to connect with certain jobs before they are widely advertised. You'll be competing for positions that most people won't even know are available.

Job seekers who stand to gain the most from insertion in computer resume databases are those who have mainstream definable education and skills—particularly technical skills—that can be measured in some way.

As one database specialist explains, "It's a lot easier to match people with 'hard' skills than people with 'soft' skills, but we do receive search orders for personnel with soft competencies, such as cultural diversity management."

Individuals who are occupationally popular in resume databanks include those in such professions as engineering, computer science, chemistry, physics, mathematics, finance, management, accounting, marketing, and human resources.

By contrast, liberal arts graduates who have failed to establish specific occupational expertise may languish in electronic limbo. Others for whom the telephone may rarely ring are those in highly specialized areas, such as fashion design, audiology, and the visual arts. As one service operator concedes, "Your name may never come up."

Job seekers with gaps in their records may avoid being penalized. Computers search for functions, performance qualifications, and total years of experience rather than for chronology. Even so, employers prefer their candidates to have a history of consistently upward movement; when a human recruiter analyzes a resume and finds unexplained voids of time, the resume customarily has been tossed.

The aversion employers have always shown to gaps in resumes may be softening as effect of the deep recession of the late 1980s and the early 1990s.

Line managers—particularly senior line managers—are most forgiving of breaks in the work history. They're often worried about their own job security and can identify with the problem of unaccounted-for months or years. Human resource staffers are somewhat understanding as well. But executive search consultants, who are retained to go after the cream of the crop on another company's payroll, may see a gap as disqualifying.

Job seekers who have obsolete skills are not good candidates for job matching through resume database services. Typists rarely are called for these days. Bookkeepers, switchboard operators, statistical clerks and bank tellers are among others whose occupations are melting down.

Why are job hunters who are out of the mainstream unlikely to turn up on a computer match? Computers can be persuaded to match criterion-for-criterion; they search for "keywords" or "descriptors."

As an example of why it's risky to rely on computer matching when you don't fit today's high-demand criteria, assume a search is begun for a medical technologist.

The keywords may include such terms as *complex laboratory tests, BS degree, cellular morphology, colorimeter,* and *spectrophotometer.*

If you are a medical technologist but have been out of the market so long that your credentials match only the first three keywords and not the last two, you probably won't wind up on any resume database's short list of candidates.

By contrast, using person-to-person networking techniques to search for a job, you may be able to persuade an employer that you're so intrinsically good it's well worth the effort to bring you aboard and "upskill" you with on-job training.

One executive search specialist speculates, "Electronic resumes are okay when looking for limited identifiable, measurable skills— particularly in a $25,000 to $75,000 range—but they do not reflect a job hunter's strength in ambition, motivation, loyalty, critical thinking, resourcefulness, and other desirable human characteristics. Computer search identifies 'things,' not personal attributes."

Admittedly, such human factors are judgment issues that can be evaluated in interviews. But, by artful statements, it's possible on paper resumes to suggest desirable traits.

A new graduate, for example, can communicate a characteristic of "determined follow-through" by commenting that he or she earned 70 percent of his or her college expenses.

Positive traits can be conveyed in documents processed through resume database systems that make available to employers a paper copy or an electronic image of the original resume. Systems that use standardized formats make it difficult, and sometimes impossible, to convey those traits.

The risk is that the exclusive use of fixed-format data can lead to premature disqualification. In cookie-cutter sameness, only core facts count. The people who have the most requested keywords rise to the top. If the job order calls for three years' experience and you have two, for instance, your name may not be plucked from electronic storage. Keep this point in mind when you are selecting an independent resume database service.

Electronic resume database services are designed to make it easy for employers to pick out the "most qualified" candidates. If your credentials, including education and experience, do not conform to the hiring criteria sought in today's job market, it's chancey to rely on computer matching to find employment.

Although you will layer your new knowledge atop your understanding of conventional methods of job finding, we advise you to assign the highest priority to mastering the high-tech job search strategies described in this book. We further recommend you study our related book, *Electronic Resume Revolution,* which offers new tactics to implement the high-tech strategies.

Electronic recruitment is the direction in which hiring is heading. Even though you've never looked for a job this way before, why not toss your hat into the resume database ring and see what happens? Especially if the listing is free.

When your credentials are in demand, a resume database service can open infinitely more doors than you may be able to open on your own.

TYPES OF RESUME DATABASE SERVICES

Although some firms focus exclusively on technical personnel, generally speaking, resume database services are not yet as specialized as employment agencies, executive recruiters, and other types of employment services.

A few firms open their doors only to recent college graduates. Others include only graduates of specific participating colleges and universities. Still others deal only with specific minority or ethnic populations.

Most are interested solely in experienced individuals. And, rather than concentrating on a narrow pool of talent, most services cover the employment spectrum A to Z.

As the industry grows, expect greater specialization because companies often use specialized resources when they attempt to fill a position. If you have skills in a specific or technical field, such as marketing or math or engineering, be certain you're listed in the resume databases most likely to act as a magnet for employers seeking people with your qualifications.

WHO SHOULD PAY FOR SHOWCASING YOU?

Because it's uncertain whether your name will ever come up in a job requisition search, *we think the only people who should pay for getting their names included in a resume database are employed people who have experience and skills to offer and who view the highly visible listing as a career management tool.*

One operator who charges for resume inclusion takes issue with this advice, making this argument: "Companies in our industry charge a registration fee as a means of assuring that higher quality resumes are submitted. In the absence of a fee, an electronic service can be perceived as a casual 'bulletin board' to which any information might be submitted.

"Charging a fee is one way to eliminate casual job seekers while enabling us to provide prospective employers with uniformly high-quality information about individuals.

"In addition, a membership fee also allows us to provide job seekers with related services, such as a newsletter of job search advice, and ongoing updating and editing of their resumes in our network. I cannot imagine a better way to focus people's best efforts on submitting information to a network than to charge them a fee for the privilege."

New graduates without work experience or steady income may develop a false sense of urgency to take any job available, through any means, in order to launch their careers.

New graduates should be wary of pressure from recruiters—or parents—to impetuously settle for a job outside their area of interest or at a lower level of employment than they could get by making a wide-angle job search.

A recruiter, for instance, may urge an undecided new graduate to accept quickly: "You're not already set in any particular field. It's a little different type of work than you had in mind—and yes, it's a little lower than your aspirations—but it's a good company. Give it a try; you might like it."

The recruiter may be correct or the recruiter may be wrong.

Some graduates go too far in the other direction—they refuse all the jobs that come within reach. Blaming poor job offers, they just can't seem to get started.

The rationale goes like this: "Well, Mom [or Dad], I read in this book that I shouldn't settle for anything less than what I really want to do. . . ." Three years later, the graduate still doesn't have a job.

No one ever blamed his or her way to success. The trick is balance—learning when to say no and when to say yes.

Be aware that there are many ways of looking for a job and an electronic database is only one of them.

A GENERAL IDEA OF HOW DATABASE SERVICES WORK

Particulars vary among services, but here's an outline of what happens to your resume once it's inserted into a database:

1. The employer's job requisition is entered into the system.
2. The computer searches for "keyword" matches to the requisition. Suppose the employer is seeking a research engineer with an advanced degree in electronics. The company operates a plant in Tijuana, Mexico, so the candidate should be able to speak fluent Spanish. Because, in lean economies, employers resist the high cost of relocating personnel, the company is particularly interested in candidates who live in San Diego County, California.

   The service's representative keyboards in these requirements, entering them via such key abbreviations and words as *MS*, *PhD*, *Electronics*, *Spanish*, and *San Diego*.

   The computer searches the database for people whose resumes match the above criteria.

   In minutes, perhaps seconds, the number of matches that contain all of the requested criteria will appear on the representative's screen.

In some systems, the matched candidates are reported alphabetically. In most systems, they are ranked against each other. For instance, a company seeking an executive with a background in finance, production, and distribution will first be presented with a slate of candidates who have those skill sets, followed by a descending-order ranking of those who have experience in only two of the target fields.

Weighting is popular in technical fields where a number of abbreviations are identified and sorted. In recruiting a chemical engineer, the candidates who know the most chemical processes required by the employer are at the top of the report; those who know the fewest are at the bottom.

3. Employers receive candidate reports. Some resume database services, in their initial report, provide only electronic capsules, which may not be to job seekers' advantage. "Too often, the computer reports make candidates blur into a blob of mayonnaise" is how one human resource manager describes computer summary reports.

In most cases, you would prefer to have a "real" resume transmitted to employers. It may be a paper version or an electronic image. It may be sent by e-mail (an electronically transmitted message) from computer to computer in the original format from which a summary was drawn.

4. The employer reviews the candidates, maybe as many as ten, and extends an interview invitation to the most promising, often three to five.

Having your resume referred to an employer through an independent resume database will not guarantee you'll be contacted by that employer. But you're certainly ahead of the pack because your qualifications meet the employer's requirements.

A HISTORY OF THE FUTURE

The archives are thin, but computerized storage of resumes appears to have begun in the mid-1960s, when the College Placement Council began operating two computerized job matching services: GRAD (Graduate Resume Accumulation and Distribution), a service for experienced professionals, and GRAD II, a service for college seniors. The systems featured the resumes of alumni and students at some 1,200 colleges and universities and made them available to more than 500 companies.

Here's How a Typical Resume Database Works

A story of maximum returns on minimum investment

It is the morning of Day 1...

Samantha Jones, vice president of a small environmental engineering and consulting firm located in Florida, calls the resume database representative:

"Hello, we're looking for a major in environmental science. This individual should have a bachelor's degree in wildlife, biology, ecology, botany, or biology."

Mike Smith, database representative:

"Let me ask you a few questions...Are you willing to look nationwide? Are you willing to relocate this candidate? What is the salary range you'll be offering? Are there any other requirements?"

On the morning of Day 3...

Mike Smith has run the search, and found qualified candidates. One of the candidates has a degree in parasitiogy, but has been working with state fish and wildlife officials during the summer months. Smith wants to know if Ms. Jones would like to talk to people who may have other good qualifications besides those she specified. Ms. Jones says yes -- Smith finalizes the search and faxes her the resumes.

The next morning

Ms. Jones is on the phone with prospective candidates. Within 45 minutes, three interviews have been set up for the following Monday morning.

Used with permission.

A recessionary economy in the early 1970s closed the service, but the software was made available to colleges to develop their own systems.

In 1981, the Career Placement Registry, a private firm operating as a subsidiary of a database producer in Alexandria, Virginia, revived the idea. Now some 1,000 client employers have access to as many as 8,000 resumes of seniors and recent graduates. A number of other companies have found niches in the electronic recruitment industry, often marketing computer resume databases.

A number of the pioneering companies did not weather economic storms and closed their doors in the 1980s. Dozens have opened and closed since the mid-1980s—in some cases, taking with them job hunters' registration fees. Perhaps they were too far ahead of their time.

Surviving firms and new start-ups have a far brighter outlook as technology moves within range for their broad success. As one entrepreneur explains, "Technology-intensive job hunting may have reached 'critical mass'—we've enough personal computers and modems to make it work now."

There's another reason electronic recruiting is an idea whose time finally has come: We live in a bottom-line economy. The bottom line of the balance sheet has become a metaphor for the conclusion that the only thing that matters is how much wealth is left after doing business.

Cost-conscious employers are beginning to balk at the cost of print advertising. Three insertions of a 2-column, 3-inch display ad in the pages of a metropolitan newspaper can cost in excess of $4,500; for the same insertions in a national business daily, the cost tops $8,400.

Employers are beginning to avoid are fees of recruitment agencies and services. Third-party fees often run into many thousands of dollars for a single hire. Fees vary widely, often ranging from as low as 1 percent to as high as 34 percent of the base salary.

Problems exist in the independent recruitment database industry. Operators must constantly promote to fill their databases with enough resumes to make them interesting for employers.

At this stage of the development of database search services, it's easier to match student and entry-level workers than older, experienced personnel. Employers are less rigid in their parameters for college seniors or other entry-level workers because they tend to view beginners as "fresh canvases" upon whom they can imprint their own organizational styles.

Employers are highly specific in their requirements for managers and seasoned professionals, which makes matchmaking a challenge. "And, to compound the difficulty of obtaining high-volume, quality matches for mid-career candidates, employers insist on certain personal qualities and intangible skills that cannot be captured on paper and therefore cannot be identified in a database search," says an East Coast resume database service owner who has wrestled with the problem.

The human factor deficiency may be resolved by technical innovations. By commanding a computer to utilize CD-ROM or other digital imaging technology—technology that is elegance itself—the human factor deficiency may be resolved by using electronic video interviewing in living color.

Just as "talkies" replaced silent films, advanced technology video interview talkies may trim the demand for silent paper resumes.

Remember, the dynamics of any new industry are fluid. The industry is literally inventing itself as you read these words. Companies enter and exit on a continuing basis.

Opening an electronic resume database service is fairly easy because it is not as capital-intensive as some other attractive business ventures and it does not require licensure. "It only takes a PC for someone to open a resume database firm," says Pete Weddle of the well-established Job Bank USA in McLean, Virginia.

As the industry matures, some companies will fail or merge—not unlike the video store industry, which was once crowded with mom-and-pop stores and is now dominated by large chains. One observer expects that either one (or a few) major resume database service will emerge, or lots of little firms will serve niche markets.

The electronic recruitment industry is unfamiliar to most of us. For your clearer understanding, we've included in this chapter a sampling of independent resume databases: their size, type, and sources of resumes; how they work; who pays the costs; the various types of client employers; and how to enter your resume, how to revise it, and how long it is retained.

We have not attempted to profile all the new resume database services springing up.

Some are limited in the occupations inventoried. An example is SS2 Online, 110 Copperwood Way, Suite A, Oceanside, CA 92054; (619)757-1055. Free to job seekers, SS2 Online is marketed to technical recruiters who, at this writing, are interested only in environmental engineers and electronic data processing personnel.

Among the services that may be limited geographically is Resumes: On-Line, 3140 K South Peoria, Suite 142, Aurora, CO 80014; (303)337-2420. This service, launched in 1992, is free to employers and is aimed at Colorado-area companies. About 150 employers search its database of some 2,000 job seekers, who pay about $30 for a four-month listing, or $40 for a one-year listing. Resumes: On-Line registers professional and managerial individuals in a wide range of career fields, from data processing and engineering to accounting and sales. Job seekers get into the database by answering ads or by signing up at outplacement centers and public job service offices.

Other limited specialized services are operated by professional societies and trade organizations. You have to be a member to be included.

Two examples of association-sponsored electronic resume databases are those open only to members of the Health Care Financial Association or the National Association of Purchasing Managers. Both databases are free to members and can be accessed for a fee by employers.

The first contains resumes of health care professionals, such as chief executive officers of hospitals and health maintenance organizations. The second contains resumes of purchasing managers. (Both of these association services are provided by NDI Services, P.O. Box 160, Northville, MI 48167.)

Ongoing visibility in a database is one more good reason why savvy career self-managers belong to professional associations.

The profiles we've chosen will help you to compare services at a glance and decide which are best for you.

If, by the time you read this book, any of the services listed have become extinct, it still will be helpful to understand how they function because similar firms—with refinements based on early experiences of pioneers—probably will have rushed in to replace them.

Whether you decide to try any of the services we discuss in this chapter or a new service you find on your own, we suggest you do the following research:

1. Get answers to these questions:

    Does this service reach the type of employers I want?

    Does this service inventory the types of jobs for which I qualify?

    How many searches per month does the service process for client employers?

    Does the service maintain statistics (not guesses) on the numbers of referrals I might expect per month?

    Is the service willing to offer suggestions on how I might improve my computer-match rate, such as revising my resume or refocusing my search?

If I must pay a fee, does the service provide a bonus period of free enroll-ment if I do not receive at least two referrals per year?

Is there an additional charge for revising or updating my resume?

Does the service provide employers with a summary of information about me? My original full resume? A standardized profile form? Is it electronically transmitted? Mailed? Faxed?

Does the service provide a list of employers currently using the data-base? (Beware of extensive lists. Half or more may be companies that haven't requested a search in months or even years. It's best to ask.)

2. Check with your local Better Business Bureau to be sure there are no negative reports. Even when you're in Topeka and the service you're considering is in New York, any Better Business Bureau can tap into its national network and request information on any company anywhere in the nation. The Bureau is into the Com-puter Age, too.

   Even when your resume is included at no charge, you want to be assured of confidentiality and the proper use of your name.

   In any industry—particularly a new one without established rules and regulations—the potential for rip-offs, scams, or just plain ineptness occurs. We've made every attempt to determine that, as of the time this book went to press, all of the services we've listed are active, legitimate, and doing what they say they'll do. Making an inquiry through a Better Business Bureau costs nothing but your time.

SAMPLING OF INDEPENDENT RESUME DATABASE SERVICES

Here is a roundup of some of the leading services. Before sending your resume or enrollment fee, it's a good idea to call any database you're considering and to confirm that its policies and prices have not changed.

▸ *Access:* 1900 West 47th Place, Suite 215, Shawnee Mission, KS 66205
   Telephone (913) 432-0700; Fax (913) 432-9451

Size and Type of Database

More than 10,000 job seekers looking for white-collar positions—from entry-level to middle management—reportedly are in the Ac-cess database. Occupational fields represented include:

Accounting	Engineering
Administration	Finance
Banking	Legal Support
Clerical	Sales
Data processing	Telemarketing

Sources of Resumes

Candidates come from multiple sources as a result of: Access advertising in local newspapers, on radio, and in trade association publications; referrals from employer client companies; and publicity generated in local media.

Unemployed and Looking for a Job Can Be Humbling

As anyone who has ever been unemployed can tell you, looking for a job is a humbling experience. "To wake up every morning and have to face the classified ads, or sit at some agency waiting for your name to be called is a major blow to your ego and your self-esteem," says Kimberly Lynk, a supervisor of credit services at a Kansas City, Missouri, bank. "You begin to question your abilities and wonder whether you will ever find employment again. Sure, you could work at a fast-food restaurant or department store, but you want a career, not just a job."

Lynk says she had been unemployed and looking for work about four months when she saw a help-wanted ad placed by Access in a Kansas City newspaper in June 1992.

"I had seen their ads before, but for some reason or other, never pursued them," recalls Lynk. "Finally, I decided to give them a try. After all, what did I have to lose?"

Two days after placing her resume into the Access database, Lynk says she received a call from Boatmen's First National Bank of Kansas City. "They had obtained a copy of my resume from Access and were interested in scheduling an interview with me," says Lynk. "I was cautiously optimistic."

Lynk explains she had her first interview about a week after entering the Access system. After being interviewed a second time the next day, she was hired.

"I was ecstatic and also amazed at how fast things had happened," she says. "My first day in my new position was just three weeks after I decided to take a chance on Access."

Commenting on the quick results, Lynk says she figures she is the exception rather than the rule, but is recommending Access to her friends.

How the System Works

1. In a double-pronged approach, a job seeker submits a resume and fills out a one-page profile form. The form supplements the resume, asking for such specifics as which three kinds of positions the job seeker would most like to have, the salary desired, and any undesirable (or required) geographic locations. The information is stored in two separate databases.

2. The information from the resume is scanned and converted to text within the computer system.

3. Employer clients contact Access by fax or telephone. Within two days, Access provides the employer with the profile information sheets and the resumes of those job seekers who most closely match the requested search criteria. The employer directly contacts job seekers for interviews.

Who Pays and How Much?

The job seeker pays a $25 processing fee for a three-month period. If the job seeker has graduated from high school or college within the past six months, the $25 fee covers six months. When a candidate finds a job through Access, the fee is refunded.

Employers pay to search the database.

Type of Client Employers

Access reportedly has about 500 employer clients ranging in size from as few as 10 employees to as many as 10,000 employees. Access is used by many industries and businesses including:

Accounting firms	Law firms
Banks	Manufacturers
Hospitals	Pharmaceutical companies

How Do You Enter Your Resume?

Mail your resume and the $25 fee to the address given above.

How Long Is a Resume Retained?

Each resume is kept active for three months (client employers want freshness as well as an indication that the job seeker is serious). For an additional $20 fee, the job seeker can renew the listing for three months.

How Do You Know if the Database Is Working for You?

One important criterion is the number of referrals you receive. Access reports that about 75 percent of the searches for employee clients result in a hire. An average of about five new employer clients per week sign up for Access services.

How Do You Revise Your Resume?

Job seekers can send a revised resume to Access at no additional charge. Access scans the updated resume and substitutes it for the original.

Other Facts

Access reports it is expanding its operation to additional cities. Access is establishing in these cities local geographic centers that will be networked together for employers and employees. Now located in Kansas City and Chicago, Access is targeting the metropolitan areas of Atlanta, Boston, Cleveland, Dallas, Denver, Minneapolis, Phoenix, and St. Louis.

Access has also launched Access Health, a related database service for health care workers, administrators, allied health and medical specialties, and nursing. This service is available in eight states: Illinois, Iowa, Kansas, Minnesota, Missouri, Nebraska, Oklahoma, and Texas.

▶ *Career Database:* 104 Mt. Auburn Street, 5th Floor, P.O. Box 2341, Cambridge, MA 02238
    Telephone (617) 876-9521; Fax (617) 661-1575

Size and Type of Database

This proprietary system is open to all job seekers. It has several thousand resumes in its database and can handle more than 1 million resumes at any given time. The system is especially attractive to employed professionals who wish to maintain marketplace visibility, because information is furnished to recruiters and employers worldwide.

Sources of Resumes

Those who learn of the service through advertising, referrals, and publicity submit their resumes for direct entry.

How the System Works

Career Database avoids misinterpretation by using only data provided by the individual candidates. It never relies on optical-character-recognition (scanning) of resumes. All resumes are different, and even keywords do not carry the same weight and meaning in differing contexts. For these reasons, Career Database says, all searches are done by using carefully developed, standardized career profiles of each individual.

1. Each job seeker fills out detailed career profile sheets in addition to any resume he or she may submit.

   Individuals who want confidentiality use a special career profile sheet that masks applicants' names, addresses, and similar information that might prematurely identify them. When a company wants additional information about a particular candidate, full disclosure is made only after specified approval is given by the applicant.

2. Employers and recruiters provide Career Database with specifications for a position.

3. Career Database personnel search for matches. Within minutes, they can compile a list of candidates' profiles that match the job requisition. The client receives a list of candidates whose profiles best match the position; names on the list are accompanied by a mini-profile of each candidate.

Who Pays and How Much?

A $50 annual membership fee is charged to the job seeker and should be sent with the resume. Employing companies and search firms may, completely free of charge, request lists of candidates for the positions they are seeking to fill.

Type of Client Employers

The database is used by companies and recruiters of all sizes, from Fortune 500 corporations to startup firms, and from large search firms to small, specialized recruiters.

How Do You Enter Your Resume?

Mail a copy of your resume and the $50 fee to the address given above.

How Long Is a Resume Retained?

A resume remains in the service's database as long as a member remains a member. Even after job seekers are placed, many of them, on an ongoing basis, continue being considered for even better jobs.

How Do You Know if the Database Is Working for You?

The service's effectiveness can be judged by the quality of the employers that subscribe to the database and the number who contact you.

How Do You Revise Your Resume?

You can update your resume and profile as many as three times a year at no additional cost. This is done quite easily. You need only mark changes on a copy of your previous profile printout.

Other Facts

Employers and search firms are provided, upon request, with two clear masters of a search request form on which to list the various specifications and requirements for the open position(s). Within a few hours—and sometimes within minutes—after the form is faxed to Career Database, a "short list" of up to ten matches, including their mini-profiles, is faxed back to the requesting employer. If no match is found, the search request is reprocessed periodically to include new resumes that have been entered in the database. Full candidate profiles are available at minimal cost to employers and recruiters upon request.

▶ **Career Placement Registry:** Career Placement Registry Inc., 302 Swann Avenue, Alexandria, VA 22301
Telephone (800) 368-3093 or (703) 683-1085; Fax (703) 683-0246

Size and Type of Database

Career Placement Registry (CPR) is an online database containing resumes of students seeking entry-level jobs and experienced personnel seeking advanced positions. The database is stored on Dialog Information Services and is available to more than 100,000 Dialog-subscribing companies and organizations located in 61 countries. Career Placement Registry contains 2,000 to 8,000 resumes during any given year.

Database Is Right Formula for New Chemical Engineer

Graduating from college isn't always a guarantee of a job. New Yorker Alan I. Goldsmith found that out the hard way. Discouraged upon graduation several years ago when few jobs were available in his field of chemical engineering, Goldsmith didn't feel it would be productive or cost-effective to send hundreds of resumes to corporate America.

Goldsmith, who now lives in Richmond, Virginia, received his bachelor's degree at The Cooper Union, a well-regarded private college in New York City. Chemical engineering offers a range of options for graduates in such fields as lubricants and fuels, flavors and fragrances, pharmaceuticals, plastics, and pulp and paper.

Aware that he was armed with only a baccalaureate and was in a soft job market, Goldsmith wasn't clear on what sort of work to seek. He opted to continue his studies at The Cooper Union, and earned the master's degree in chemical engineering.

Goldsmith's qualifications included broad training in engineering and mathematics, experience in searching chemical literature indexed by the American Chemical Society's Chemical Abstracts Service, and proficiency with the Unix computer operating system.

As Goldsmith neared completion of his master's program, once again his thoughts turned to launching his career.

"Sitting through job placement seminars and listening to the few students who had managed to find summer engineering jobs, I realized the futility of trying to tell campus recruiters that I was just the person for the job," Goldsmith recalls. "In fact, the more I thought about it, the more I realized that a better fit would be obtained if I laid out my qualifications and let prospective employers do the matching. They could judge better than I whether I met their particular requirements."

Goldsmith submitted a copy of his resume to the American Chemical Society (ACS) National Employment Clearinghouse, and also signed up with Career Placement Registry (CPR), a resume database firm in Alexandria, Virginia. CPR had included an application in a mailing from the society's employment clearinghouse.

While he was editing his master's thesis in July 1988, Goldsmith says, he received a telephone call from a Fortune 500 company that was attempting to fill a new position in its literature searching group.

The company had accessed his resume through CPR's database. Goldsmith figures it was his experience in searching chemical literature and his knowledge of the Unix computer operating system that made his resume "jump out" at the hiring manager.

The employment offer was made and accepted. Goldsmith says he feels fortunate to have been hired because at that time not too many chemical engineering jobs in industry were available.

"In this position, I respond to questions in all areas of engineering and technology, primarily by searching electronic databases," explains the young chemical engineer. "Moreover, my Unix skills have been put to good use to enhance significantly my editing and formatting of search results."

"It was through the Career Placement Registry that the perfect match came looking for me," Goldsmith explains. "It is enormously satisfying being told your services are needed, and I pass on the same compliment to CPR."

Sources of Resumes

Some resumes are obtained through ads in media such as school newspapers and personnel magazines. Other resumes are forwarded from commercial resume print shops, college career centers, and personnel agencies, often as a result of word-of-mouth recommendations.

How the System Works

1. Individuals complete the CPR data entry forms, which are then computerized by CPR. A copy is returned to each person for verification.
2. The data are loaded into the Dialog (discussed in Chapter 4) service on a weekly basis.
3. After six months, a letter is sent to the individual indicating a date when the person will be dropped from the database. The job seeker has the option to renew or update the data entry form and continue the service for another six months.

Who Pays and How Much?

Both individuals and employers pay. The exact amount varies. Students pay $15. Experienced persons pay as follows: Up to $20,000 salary, $25; $20,001 to $40,000 salary, $35; $40,001 or over, $45. Employer clients pay to search the database.

Type of Client Employers

Fortune 1000 companies, including insurance companies, banks, industrial companies, government agencies, and nonprofit organizations, access the database. Some 1,500 companies and organizations are CPR clients.

How Do You Enter Your Resume?

Call and request a data entry form. Return the completed form with a check or money order for the appropriate amount to the address given above.

How Long Is a Resume Retained?

A resume is retained for six months after the data appear on DIALOG Information Services.

How Do You Know if the Database Is Working for You?

Because all clients have a confidential password with DIALOG, CPR cannot report on the number of hires. CPR does monitor the number of resumes extracted from the database each month, which indicates usage.

How Do You Revise Your Resume?

Changes forwarded directly to Career Placement Registry will be loaded into the databases during the next update.

Other Facts

Career Placement Registry provides the ability to communicate with thousands of companies seeking employees. The cost is a fraction of the amount an individual would spend to mail printed resumes. CPR clients have been introduced to the system and know how to search the system.

▶ *cors:* One Pierce Place, Suite 300 East, Itasca, IL 60143
Telephone (800) 323-1352 or (708) 250-8677; Fax (708) 250-7362

Size and Type of Database

This Chicago-based service boasts more than 1.5 million resumes. When researching the database, cors has the capacity to sort in a myriad of ways, which makes it unlikely that any appropriately qualified individuals are overlooked. Both entry-level and seasoned individuals in all fields are in the database.

Networking contacts are used to enhance database searches. If the research doesn't reveal an appropriate candidate, cors research analysts contact the nearest matches and keep networking until they identify individuals who are close matches to the job requisition.

Sources of Resumes

Resumes are received by cors from a variety of channels, including direct telephone calls, referrals, universities, trade shows, and businesses attempting to place workers who are to be laid off.

How the System Works

1. This service takes assignments from employer clients. Job specifications are a starting point for every networking assignment and database search.
2. Once the resumes have been selected, cors personnel contact each individual job seeker to determine interest in the client's opportunity.
3. Once an individual is hired by a cors client, his or her name and resume are purged from the database.

Who Pays and How Much?

The job seeker pays a $25 processing fee to have a resume entered into the cors database. The employer clients, who reportedly number more than 5,800, pay cors a fee to research and identify qualified professionals.

Type of Client Employers

Clients of cors reportedly consist of organizations in most vertical markets, including manufacturing, financial, insurance, retail, transportation, health care, computer consulting, telecommunications, and service-oriented companies. Clients reportedly range from small businesses to Fortune 500 companies.

How Do You Enter Your Resume?

Call cors toll-free (except in Illinois) and give the representative your name and brief history over the phone. You can then fax or mail your complete resume and a check for $25 to the address given above. Cors will enter your resume and confirm the process via telephone or mail.

How Long Is a Resume Retained?

According to cors, a resume is retained indefinitely. Within the database, cors separates the resumes according to the length of time since the last contact by a cors representative for a position. The resume is placed in an inactive file when an individual cannot be located at a work or home address.

How Do You Know if the Database Is Working for You?

According to cors officials, database performance depends on client need and the quality of the resume supplied by the applicant. The submitted information should be as direct and informative as possible. The more a person is open to relocating, the greater number of chances he or she will be contacted by cors.

How Do You Revise Your Resume?

Revisions of data are simple. After payment for entry of the original resume ($25), the job seeker receives a designated note number for updating purposes. The individual can submit any changes via telecommunications (telephone or fax) or in writing. All correspondence should be directed to the cors Client Services Department. There is no charge for the updating service.

Other Facts

In what may be a breakthrough service in this industry, cors will conduct a unique job search for the job seeker upon entering his or her resume into the system. For an additional $50 fee, cors will match the resume, with help-wanted ads in 70 leading newspapers, as well as with openings in its client base.

▸ **DORS (Defense Outplacement Referral System):** Operation Transition, DMDC, 99 Pacific Street, Suite 155-A, Monterey, CA 93940
    Telephone (800) 727-3677; Fax (408) 656-2132

Size and Type of Database

The DORS database is designed to provide the nation's employers with access to service members (and their spouses) who are leaving the armed forces. More than 10,000 resumes are online. A part of the U.S. Department of Defense's Operation Transition, DORS was established in late 1991, and can be used by the more than 300,000 armed forces personnel (and their spouses) who annually separate from active duty. This mainframe/PC database is open to all employers who register with the Department of Defense, either directly or through one of the Department of Defense transition offices around the world.

Sources of Resumes

Military personnel (and their spouses) who are about to end their active duty careers and re-enter civilian life sign up with DORS.

How the System Works

1. Service members and their spouses voluntarily enter a mini-resume (a standardized profile form), which specifies their experience, education, type of job, and geographic preferences.
2. Employers register by calling the 800 number given above. Once registered, employers receive instructional materials on DORS. After that, they can request specific matches of personnel.
3. The DORS system matches the mini-resumes with the job and geographic specifications requested by employers through a touch-tone telephone system.
4. Employers access DORS by calling a 900 telephone number.
5. Employers can receive up to 25 mini-resumes by fax the same business day, or up to 100 resumes by mail the next business day.

Who Pays and How Much?

The DORS service is free to service personnel and their spouses. Employers pay $5 for the first minute via the 900 telephone number, and $1 per minute thereafter.

Type of Client Employers

Nearly 4,000 employers—the number is increasing by 100 to 200 per month—across the nation are registered with Operation Transition. They are making more than 600 requests monthly. Employers using DORS range from small businesses to Fortune 500 companies and from high-tech to blue-collar occupations. They are at locations across the nation as well as overseas. They regularly offer exiting military personnel and their spouses jobs such as:

Computer programmer	Long-distance truckdriver
Electronics repairer	Manager
Financial representative	Police officer
Guard	Sales engineer
Health care professional	School teacher
Insurance sales worker	Secretary

How Do You Enter Your Resume?

Active duty personnel and their spouses can register for the DORS program by completing an Operation Transition registration form at their local military installation transition office. Transition professionals offer assistance in completing the form, if needed. Once the form is filled out, it is input on an Operation Transition PC and uploaded to the DORS mainframe computer in Monterey, California.

How Long Is a Resume Retained?

DORS maintains a resume in its database for as long as 90 days after separation.

How Do You Know if the Database Is Working for You?

Considering the limits that active duty places on military personnel, particularly if they are stationed overseas prior to separation, job seekers have nothing to lose by inserting their resumes into the DORS system. DORS officials report that they continue to poll both service personnel and employers, to get results of successes from both sides.

How Do You Revise Your Resume?

DORS officials recommend that job seekers register at transition offices within 90 days before separation. Just before separation day, job seekers are advised to update their resume one final time, making it good for another 90 days. When the 90-day period after separation has expired, the resume is eliminated from the DORS system.

Other Facts

DORS job seekers gain further exposure to employers through the U.S. Department of Labor's Interstate Job Bank, a network among public job service offices. DORS mini-resumes are provided to all states that list job openings on the Interstate Job Bank. The states, in turn, may refer the mini-resumes to appropriate local employers.

▶ *Electronic Job Matching:* 1915 N. Dale Mabry Highway, Suite 307, Tampa, FL 33607
Telephone (800) 749-4100 or (813) 879-4100; Fax (813) 870-1883

Size and Type of Database

Electronic Job Matching (a service of Human Resource Management Center, Inc.) says it is a computerized database/decision support system that documents job candidates' credentials and preferences much more comprehensively than does a resume alone. Employers can dial directly into the computer system to do their own searches.

The service uses both a resume supplied by the individual and a supplemental sheet listing job-specific skills, proficiencies, and other information on abilities that the candidate may possess but did not include in his or her resume. Electronic Job Matching (EJM) reports that this extra effort helps make sure an individual possessing the background specified by an employer will not be overlooked simply because a keyword or phrase was left out of the resume.

EJM is composed of many different online services and databases tailored to serve the diverse needs and interests of various job seekers and employers. Collectively, many thousands of job applicants are represented in the system. Individual smaller databases permit highly focused representation for each job applicant.

Sources of Resumes

EJM reports that it is designed to serve the interests of many different types of career professionals and groups of employers. Applicants come from a wide variety of sources.

Job seekers are referred to EJM by professionals already in the system, employers using the system, civic associations, alumni associations, colleges, vocational-technical schools, trade associations, professional resume writing firms, outplacement firms, career expos, job fairs, minority groups, and women's associations.

How the System Works

1. EJM creates an electronic portfolio for each job seeker. The portfolio represents the person's career objective and talents in far more detail than would a resume alone.

2. A job seeker's portfolio is stored on EJM's computer and is available to every employer with a computer.

    When confidentiality is important, the job seeker's identity is kept private, by coding, until a legitimate employer interest is established. Names, addresses, and the names of current and previous employers are withheld until a prospective employer's interest is confirmed. As a further safeguard, a job seeker may block any specific employer from ever viewing his or her profile, no matter how ideal the match.

3. Upon receiving search orders, EJM guides employers through the process of determining their search criteria. Because employers are given direct access to appropriate job seeker portfolios, they make their own slate of selections. Note one important point: Even though employers have direct access to job seekers, only those portfolios that match—and are not otherwise blocked by the job seeker's request—are presented for employer review. No employer has indiscriminate access to all job candidates.

Employers, when accessing EJM, are asked for such information as job-specific skills with desired proficiency level, industry background wanted, maximum salary to be offered, minimum years of education, work experience required, relocation factors.

Because job seekers are asked for similar information to supplement their resumes, the accuracy of the match can be much greater and the likelihood of overlooking an appropriate candidate is minimized.

Who Pays and How Much?

The EJM service is free to individual job seekers. Employers pay a fee based on time connected to the system and, in some cases, the number of profiles selected. The average employer's search takes about five minutes.

Type of Client Employers

Each database services specific job seeker interests and categories of employers and industries. Employers include both small and large entities. This is a brief sampling of industries served:

Banking	Manufacturing
Business services	Medicine
Data processing	Publishing
High technology	Service industries

How Do You Enter Your Resume?

Mail your resume, and an indication of the kinds of positions for which you'd like to be considered, to the address given above.

An EJM job seeker packet with supplemental forms will be returned to you for completion (takes about 20 minutes). Within 24 hours of receipt of the forms, your electronic portfolio will be available to employers throughout your local community and nationwide, as you desire.

To access the system, employers first must contact EJM (at one of the telephone numbers listed above) to obtain a unique set of passwords and instructions on how to use the system (at no charge).

How Long Is a Resume Retained?

Electronic portfolios, which include the resumes, are kept active and online until job seekers are hired, or for a period of four months. Your listing may be extended for additional four-month periods free of charge, but you must contact EJM and request the extension(s).

How Do You Know if the Database Is Working for You?

EJM says it can track the number of times an individual's portfolio is reviewed or requested, and can report this information to the job seeker. The job seeker can discuss the composition of his or her resume and supplemental information with an EJM representative and get suggestions on ways to boost the frequency of matching. Plans include a periodic publication for job seekers. It will report on the kinds of positions employers are seeking to fill, together with specific criteria requested, salary ranges, and other details, so that job seekers can compare their credentials with employers' requirements.

How Do You Revise Your Resume?

Your resume, as well as any of the additional information gathered about your credentials, can be updated at any time simply by notifying EJM by mail of the changes.

Other Facts

EJM has been chosen as one of the top 20 new human resources services in the nation by a human resource trade journal. EJM also is utilized in the Educational Testing Services' WORKLINK national school-to-work transition service, and in the Urban Leadership Career Network sponsored by *Urban Business* magazine.

▶ ***HispanData:*** 360 S. Hope Avenue, Suite 300-C, Santa Barbara, CA 93105
    Telephone (805) 682-5843; Fax (805) 687-4546

Size and Type of Database

Between 5,000 and 6,000 resumes of Hispanic college-educated individuals are in HispanData at any given time. The service offers a spectrum of professional and managerial fields, including:

Computer science	Mathematics
Engineering	Physics
Finance management	Sales
Marketing	

Positions are mid-level, requiring three to five years' experience, or entry level for new college graduates. A 3.0 grade point average is required for new graduates but not for experienced job seekers.

Sources of Resumes

Candidates come to HispanData as a result of:

1. Advertising that solicits resumes, in *Hispanic Business* magazine.
2. Hispanic organizations, such as National Society of Hispanic MBAs, Society of Hispanic Professional Engineers, and Hispanic Organization of Professionals and Executives.
3. New graduates of some 250 colleges and universities.
4. Word-of-mouth referrals.

How the System Works

1. Employers provide HispanData with job specifications for each position.
2. HispanData personnel search the resume database to identify qualified candidates.
3. HispanData personnel call each potential candidate to prescreen the job fit as well as to verify availability and interest in the opening.

4. HispanData provides employers with a paper resume for each qualified candidate. The salary issue varies: A pay range for the position may or may not be revealed, or an applicant's salary requirements may or may not be requested.

5. Employers contact potential candidates to arrange for interviews.

Who Pays and How Much?

Job seekers pay a one-time $15 listing fee to the service. Employers purchase annual contracts from HispanData.

Type of Client Employers

Fortune 1000 corporations, nonprofit organizations, and government agencies that desire to achieve diversity or meet affirmative action goals subscribe to HispanData.

How Do You Enter Your Resume?

Verify that there are no changes in requirements by calling Hispan-Data. Along with a $15 check, send a single copy of your resume to the address given above.

How Long Is a Resume Retained?

Each resume remains in the database for life; HispanData sends update forms every six months.

How Do You Know if the Database Is Working for You?

HispanData is a long-term commitment; evaluate its effectiveness by the number of referrals you receive.

How Do You Revise Your Resume?

Contact HispanData by mail, sending a revised resume.

Other Facts

HispanData is reportedly the leading database of Hispanic professionals, who generally are bilingual.

▶ *Job Bank USA:* 1420 Spring Hill Road, Suite 480, McLean, VA 22102
Telephone (800) 296-1USA; Fax (703) 847-1494

Size and Type of Database

Job Bank USA says it has inventories of more than 17,000 resumes at
any one time. It is a nationwide, comprehensive, all-purpose recruiting resource filled with resumes of individuals in all occupations, at
all experience levels, across all industries and service sectors.
Sample job titles are:

Attorney	Manufacturing manager
Benefits administrator	Mortgage broker
Buyer/merchandiser	Office manager
Chief executive officer	Paralegal
Chief financial officer	Programmer
Design engineer	Restaurant manager
Director of nursing	Sales representative
Executive vice president	Secretary
Industrial hygienist	Tax assistant
Logistics coordinator	Vice president
Marketing manager	Wellness manager

Sources of Resumes

Resumes are received by Job Bank USA from individuals who discovered the database through:

1. Leading professional and technical societies, trade associations,
   and alumni associations of academic institutions. Examples are
   the Society for Human Resource Management, the American College of Health Care Administrators, the Institution of Certified
   Financial Planners, the National Office Products Association, the
   University of Notre Dame, the Universities of California and
   Texas, and the United States Military Academy.
2. National, regional, and local outplacement companies.
3. Affinity groups (including fraternities, sororities, and clubs),
   military personnel worldwide, career counseling firms, and employment support groups.

How the System Works

1. Individuals complete a short enrollment form and attach their resume or employment record to enter their qualifications in the

Out of Uniform, into a Job

Resume databases can work effectively for long-distance searches, for newcomers, or for returning service personnel, as in the case of former U.S. Marine Lee Ann Bailey of Alexandria, Virginia.

Bailey says she found herself facing displacement after four years of service. Her most recent assignment was in California, but given the economic climate and difficulties of finding a position, she decided to return to her hometown on the East Coast to pursue employment in the private sector.

"I found retail sales positions to be in abundance; however, I felt the skills I acquired during my tenure in the Marine Corps were more suited to an accounting/administrative environment," says Bailey. "I pursued all available leads, including classified advertising, placement services, and the local employment commission."

Bailey says an interviewer at the employment commission suggested she try Job Bank USA, a resume database service in McLean, Virginia.

"I called Job Bank USA and was provided with an overview of their services and was sent by mail an enrollment form to complete and return with my resume," Bailey recalls. "Within ten days of my enrollment being activated, I received three calls from one of the Job Bank USA recruiters."

During all telephone calls, Bailey was given a description of the position listed and the opportunity to consent to her resume being sent to a corporate client.

"Two of the positions presented to me were a comfortable match and I agreed to have my resume forwarded," says Bailey. "The position in which I was especially interested was with a large real estate organization—in its accounting department."

Bailey says she was happy to discover the real estate company also considered her a match and, after two interviews, she was offered the position.

"I recommend Job Bank USA to anyone searching for employment," said Bailey. "It proved to be a very effective career marketing resource."

Job Bank USA database. Individuals are contacted within ten days to confirm enrollment; they are given a toll-free telephone number for updating their records.

2. Employers purchase annual subscriptions for a specified number of job searches. For each search, employers call a telephone number and provide job specifications to a professional recruiter on the Job Bank USA staff. The recruiter searches the database to identify qualified candidates.

3. Job Bank USA recruiters call each qualified candidate to verify qualifications and availability, as well as interest in the job opening. Enrollment records of the qualified candidates are updated and augmented to reflect new information about the candidates that is relevant to the open position.

4. Job Bank USA does not refer an individual's record to a prospective employer without the individual's permission. The prepermission policy is designed to avoid wasting employers' time with individuals who are not serious candidates and to preserve the privacy of an individual's career management or job-seeking activities.

5. Employers are contacted by a Job Bank USA recruiter within 48 hours of ordering a database search and are given the status of qualified, prescreened candidates.

Who Pays and How Much?

Job seekers pay an annual fee of $30 to enroll in what the company terms the "Career Advancement Service." In addition to the database enrollment, the fee includes quarterly issues of a newsletter about job search trends and tips, and a catalog of career books and guidance materials. Employers pay for searches.

Type of Client Employers

More than 350 active client employers, ranging in size from major international corporations and Fortune 500 firms to regional and local employers, search the database.

How Do You Enter Your Resume?

Call and request an enrollment form. (Mention this book and receive a 10 percent discount.)

How Long Is a Resume Retained?

Enrollment forms are retained in the Job Bank USA database for one year. Many individuals renew their enrollments.

How Do You Know if the Database Is Working for You?

Job Bank USA says it is conducting more than 100 job searches per day for employers. More than 60 percent of the individuals referred to these employers by Job Bank USA receive face-to-face interviews. If you feel you're not getting your fair share of referrals, call the Job Bank USA Recruiting Center at the number listed above and ask recruiters to review your resume. Job Bank USA recruiters will help database enrollees generally improve their resumes and strengthen them for specific positions for which an individual may be referred.

How Do You Revise Your Resume?

Each person enrolled in the Job Bank USA database is given a telephone number to use in making unlimited updates and changes to the enrollment form.

Other Facts

Job Bank USA says its philosophy favors long-term career management over short-term emergency job finding.

Job Bank USA is one of the most active resume database firms in operation. Positions are appropriate for experienced individuals seeking better jobs, recent college graduates, veterans transitioning into the civilian market, work-ready persons with disabilities, returners to the job market, and others who have marketable skills.

▶ *kiNexus:* P.O. Box 803818, Chicago, IL 60680
   Telephone (800) 828-0422, ext. 200; Fax (312) 642-0616

Size and Type of Database

This Chicago-based service is said to publish a database containing 175,000 resumes of active employment candidates—65 percent new college graduates and 35 percent experienced professionals.

Sources of Resumes

Reportedly, more than half of the nation's 3,600 two- and four-year colleges and universities can register their graduates in kiNexus at no charge. Registration programs also are in effect with numerous alumni and professional associations, as well as other special interest groups. In addition, for a fee, individuals can enter resumes into the database.

How the System Works

1. Subscribing employers access the kiNexus resume database through their own PCs. They can choose from the entire database on CD-ROM technology. (kiNexus is thought to be the nation's only CD-ROM database publisher.)

   Employers also contact kiNexus to conduct "On-Call" searches, which means kiNexus employees will do the legwork in selecting a slate of suitable candidates to forward to the employer.

   When resumes are coded, kiNexus personnel must intervene for the match process to continue; job seekers may not wish to have their resumes sent to certain employers—like their own bosses.

2. In either instance, whenever the employer's requirements match the job seeker's qualifications, the candidate's electronic resume automatically pops up.

3. Candidates are contacted by employers when there is a match.

Who Pays and How Much?

New college graduates register free. At some colleges and universities, the no-charge policy continues for up to 12 months. Experienced candidates pay according to their affinity group.

Experienced candidates who are otherwise unaffiliated with a kiNexus registration program pay $30 to register in the database. The confidentiality option costs an additional $20.

Employers pay a subscription fee to access the database.

Type of Client Employers

kiNexus serves large and small corporations, both national and international, as well as nonprofit organizations and governmental agencies.

How Do You Enter Your Resume?

Sign up at participating college career centers by filling out registration forms. Some colleges provide an IBM-PC-compatible kiNexus

When You Have a Job but Want a Better One

Good things don't always happen quickly. Aleksandar Stojanovski entered his resume with kiNexus just before graduation, when the Chicago database service was recommended to him by a counselor in his college's career center.

Stojanovski, a native of Belgrade, Yugoslavia, is living the American dream of thousands of immigrants before him. He graduated in the early 1990s from Oakland University in Rochester, Michigan, where he received his bachelor's degree in electrical engineering.

A standout student, Stojanovski was senior class president and a whiz in mathematics, computers, and basketball. His college grade point average was 3.5; his summers and times between semesters were filled with a variety of job experiences working for a major automaker, a large cable communications company, a plastics firm, and a state agency.

After graduation, the young electrical engineer took a job in computer programming. The job was not found through kiNexus and it was not what Stojanovski really wanted to do.

Time passed. He almost forgot about his resume being included in the kiNexus database. Despite receiving academic and departmental honors at Oakland University, Stojanovski didn't get a single response from having his profile in the kiNexus database—until 14 months after graduation. Then the call came. "Eureka!," Stojanovski thought. It was a job he really wanted.

"I had nearly forgotten about even being in the system, until I got a call from Electronic Data Systems in Troy, Michigan," says Stojanovski. "I knew EDS must have heard about me from kiNexus because I had not applied to them myself."

Stojanovski remembers that after three interviews he was offered a job as a programmer in the company's engineering systems development department.

"I think EDS became interested in me because of a combination of my work experience and my grade point average in college," said Stojanovski.

He thinks kiNexus is a good idea. "If someone asks me my opinion, I'm giving it a big thumbs up."

preprogrammed computer diskette, which guides the job seeker through the complete questionnaire.

Some affinity groups have processing arrangements with kiNexus; if you are a member of one that does, you'll be notified through that group's membership bulletins.

Individuals not otherwise eligible can enter directly by contacting kiNexus. Company officials say it is recommended that job seekers first purchase an IBM-PC-compatible kiNexus preprogrammed computer diskette package, to help with filling out the questionnaire. This package currently costs $19.95; the package fee does not count toward the fee for being inserted in the database.

How Long Is a Resume Retained?

Information remains in the kiNexus database for a year from its date of entry, which is about two weeks after the job seeker sends in the registration form. Unless the service receives an individual's request to re-register, the information is removed at the end of the one-year period.

How Do You Know if the Database Is Working for You?

The quality of the employers that subscribe to the database and the number who contact you will give you this feedback.

How Do You Revise Your Resume?

During the current period of registration, you can update your resume information at any time for $10 per update.

Other Facts

Founded in 1987, kiNexus is thought to be one of the largest resume database services in the United States. kiNexus says it is the only electronic employment information service that publishes its database. Most employers ask kiNexus to conduct their searches for them. kiNexus calls every candidate selected, to verify interest in the position, before turning names over to employers. This minimizes inappropriate referrals for employers and false hopes for candidates. Many employers reportedly are using kiNexus to identify student candidates for summer jobs, internships, and other part-time opportunities. These positions strengthen resumes and build relationships that can lead to full-time employment upon graduation.

▶ *National Resume Bank:* 3637 4th Street North, No. 330, St.
Petersburg, FL 33704
    Telephone (813) 896-3694; Fax (813) 894-1277

Size and Type of Database

The National Resume Bank is an online resume database currently
listing more than 3,000 job candidates in 22 different career categories.

Sources of Resumes

The National Resume Bank is a service of the Professional Association of Resume Writers, which has more than 600 member offices
throughout the United States and Canada. Job But
seekers can get into this database through any participating association member, or by contacting the association's headquarters.

How the System Works

1. The National Resume Bank is compatible with both IBM and
   Macintosh systems, and with 2400-baud modems.
2. The system is user-friendly and requires no special software.
3. Employers dial the National Resume Bank modem line (813) 822-
   7082 and select from 22 job categories the one that most closely
   describes the job opening. They can then select the geographic
   parameters desired (city, state, or national search).
4. Employers are shown a brief qualifications summary on each current job candidate who meets the search criteria.
5. Employers can contact the candidate directly or, with a keystroke, order a paper copy of the candidate's resume.

    After an employer logs on to the system the first time, the data-
base will recognize the company name for future searches. For example, an employer who may not wish to review every resume
during each search can ask to see only the new listings since the last
search.

Who Pays and How Much?

Job candidates pay $25 for a three-month listing or $40 for unlimited
time until they are employed or they request removal from the database. The service is free to employers.

Type of Client Employers

Because National Resume Bank does not require special employer software or charge prepaid, online, or download fees, the service is more accessible to small employers as well as to Fortune 500 companies. With 90 percent of new jobs being created by companies with fewer than 100 employees, the National Resume Bank says it is particularly user-friendly to this vast employment market.

The National Resume Bank is open to job applicants in 22 different categories:

Aerospace	General
Airlines	Government/public service
Casino (gaming)	Health care
Clerical	Hospitality
Communications	Legal
Creative	Management
Data processing	Manufacturing
Education	Real estate
Engineering/technical	Retail
Entertainment	Sales
Financial	Trades

(New categories may be added and current titles modified or deleted in response to future market needs and interests.)

How Do You Enter Your Resume?

Contact a local member of the Professional Association of Resume Writers (see your yellow pages directory), or mail five copies of your resume along with the $25 or $40 listing fee to the address given above.

How Long Is a Resume Retained?

Each resume is kept three or six months, initially, depending on the length of the listing purchased. A listing may be renewed prior to expiration.

After each selected period on the database, the National Resume Bank mails database members a management report. The report notifies each job seeker how many times his or her listing was viewed by employers and how many times the full resume was requested.

At the same time, job seekers should be alert to direct contact by employers. A National Resume Bank listing includes the individual's telephone number and address (unless an individual requests that his or her information be "hidden"), and encourages an employer to immediately contact a suitable prospect for a telephone interview or appointment.

How Do You Know if the Database Is Working for You?

You know by the quality of the employers who subscribe to the database and the number who contact you.

How Do You Revise Your Resume?

This can be done at any time by sending National Resume Bank five copies of the new resume with a $5 update fee.

Other Facts

The National Resume Bank was begun in October 1991 as a new client service for members of the Professional Association of Resume Writers. It is designed to help job seekers present their qualifications and credentials to the 80 percent of employers who don't advertise their job openings in local classified ads.

During 1992 (National Resume Bank's first full year), listed resumes received more than 50,000 viewings by employers with current job openings.

▶ _**Resumes-On-Computer:**_ Curtis Development Company, 1000 Waterway Boulevard, Indianapolis, IN 46202
Telephone (317) 636-1000; Fax (317) 634-1791

Size and Type of Database

Operated by Curtis Development Company, in Indianapolis, Resumes-On-Computer (ROC) is a database of more than 3,300 resumes. They are made available to more than 2,700 employer client subscribers of the Human Resource Information Network, the nation's only online service designed specifically for the use of corporate human resource professionals (the people who find and screen new hires).

Sources of Resumes

Candidates come from multiple sources as a result of outplacement firms, resume writing firms, quick-printing companies, trade associations, college placement services, and vocational schools.

How the System Works

Entry of resumes is done primarily through a quick-print shop or resume writing firm that is equipped with the ROC Resume Entry Program. You can have your resume created at one of these neighborhood shops or firms in the traditional way. The ROC program "tags" each resume with certain job-seeker-defined preferences. This helps employer clients find appropriate resumes.

The ROC Resume Entry Program:

1. Converts any word-processed resume file into a format suitable for computerized searching. Once converted, resumes are copied onto a blank diskette, submitted to ROC, and immediately listed in its database.
2. Allows existing resumes to be edited or new resumes to be created. The program also offers the option of listing a resume anonymously.
3. Assists in answering career-specific questions. Job seekers' responses are appended to their resumes, to aid employers in locating appropriate applicants.
4. Displays a converted resume on the screen as it will appear to employers.
5. Can be used with any DOS-based or Macintosh computer.

Who Pays and How Much?

ROC recommends that printers charge job seekers no more than $10 for a listing. Subscribing employers pay a fee to the Human Resource Information Network to access ROC.

Type of Client Employers

Some 80 percent of Fortune 500 company human resource offices have passwords to the Human Resource Information Network and hence access to ROC.

How Do You Enter Your Resume?

Contact a nearby quick-print shop or resume writing firm and ask if it inputs to ROC. If not, suggest that the shop or firm creating your resume call ROC for a free copy of the ROC resume entry software.

You can contact ROC directly at the address given above.

To finalize entry into ROC, you will be asked by the printer to sign a resume release form, which is submitted to ROC along with the diskette.

How Long Is a Resume Retained?

ROC will keep your resume online for six months.

How Do You Know if the Database Is Working for You?

The quality of the employers who subscribe to the database and the number of contacts you receive will give you a clue.

How Do You Revise Your Resume?

To update an existing resume, it is necessary to delete the old one and submit a new one, again paying the listing fee.

Other Facts

All resumes listed on ROC are also listed on the Career Placement Registry database, described earlier in this chapter.

ROC does not routinely confirm the receipt of resume diskettes. Those job seekers wishing confirmation should send their resume diskettes to ROC by certified mail, return receipt requested. Alternatively, ROC will confirm the listing on ROC of any resume as long as the interested job seeker makes this request in writing.

Job seekers and employers wishing to obtain a password for direct computerized access to ROC resumes should contact the Human Resource Information Network at (800) 421-8884.

▶ *SkillSearch:* 104 Woodmont Boulevard, Suite 306, Nashville, TN 37205

Telephone (800) 252-5665; Fax (615) 383-4743

Size and Type of Database

SkillSearch is a computerized career networking service linking college alumni and potential employers. The service is sponsored by more than 60 participating university alumni associations. SkillSearch targets all alumni of participating universities. The network's membership represents a complete range of experience, from junior level to seasoned executives.

Sources of Resumes

Alumni of participating colleges and universities sign up.

How the System Works

1. Alumni are solicited directly by mail.
2. Participating alumni in the SkillSearch network complete an application that is transformed into a professional resume and unique data record.
3. The partnership with the participating university alumni associations provides SkillSearch with a database of skilled professionals ready to fill open positions.
4. Employers pay a fee for a database search that allows contact with up to 20 matching prospective candidates.
5. The employers select the profiles they wish to explore further.

Who Pays and How Much?

Alumni join SkillSearch for a one time fee of $65; renewals are $15 per year. Employers pay for a search of the database. If no matching candidates are found, the employer pays nothing.

Type of Client Employers

Fortune 1000 corporations, nonprofit organizations, and governmental agencies, as well as small- to medium-size companies, are clients of SkillSearch.

How Do You Enter Your Resume?

Alumni register with SkillSearch. Check with your office of alumni affairs for further information, or contact SkillSearch at the address given above.

How Long Is a Resume Retained?

Information remains in the database for one year and is renewable with payment of the annual fee.

How Do You Know if the Database Is Working for You?

You can judge the effectiveness of the database by the quality of the subscribing employers and the quantity of contacts you receive.

How Do You Revise Your Resume?

Updates can be made as often as desired by notifying SkillSearch.

Other Facts

SkillSearch works only with alumni who have at least two years' work experience. The average is ten years. SkillSearch does not accept resumes from students.

▶ **University ProNet:** 3803 East Bayshore Road, Box 51820, Palo Alto, CA 94303
      Telephone: see below; Fax (415) 691-1619

Size and Type of Database

University ProNet is a private company wholly owned and operated by the 11 participating universities—all national leaders in the fields of business, engineering, science, law, medicine, and biotechnology. The database consists of 40,000 alumni of these universities.

The service is designed for professionals who have two or more years of experience. The preponderance of opportunities is in middle- to senior-level positions. Some 20 percent of individuals in the database are thought to be actively on the job market; 80 percent are open to career advancement moves.

More than 77 percent of individuals in the database hold advanced degrees, and more than 33 percent are currently employed as senior executives. Ten years is the median experience.

Participating institutions are: California Institute of Technology, Carnegie-Mellon University, Massachusetts Institute of Technology, Ohio State University, Stanford University, University of California at Berkeley, University of California at Los Angeles, University of Illinois, University of Michigan, University of Texas at Austin, and Yale University.

Sources of Resumes

The database is restricted to alumni of participating universities.

How the System Works

1. Employers subscribe to the service on an annual basis. The level of subscription purchased determines the number of searches they can request.
2. When a search order is received, University ProNet personnel search the database and call likely candidates with whom to discuss the position.
3. Profiles of qualified alumni who are interested in the position—identified by code number only—are then forwarded to the client company.
4. The company identifies the specific candidates it would like to interview. At this point, University ProNet staff release to the company the identity and contact information for each candidate and notify the candidates of the action.
5. Employers contact candidates directly. University ProNet staff now work as agents for the alumni, functioning as liaisons throughout the interviewing process.

To make its electronic service even more valuable, University ProNet publishes a twice-monthly resume book of alumni (different job seekers appear in each issue), and produces a twice-monthly printed job bulletin of employment opportunities apart from those filled through the electronic search system.

Who Pays and How Much?

Alumni are charged a lifetime fee of $35 to register in the program and be cross-matched against searches initiated by the subscribing companies.

Individuals who choose to have their profiles circulated in the resume book mailing and to receive the job bulletin for six months pay an additional $25.

Companies subscribe to University ProNet on an annual basis.

Type of Client Employers

A cross-section of business, financial, medical, legal, engineering, and consumer product corporations and organizations are clients.

How Do You Enter Your Resume?

University ProNet is a service of each school's alumni association to its alumni. Units are called, for example, Stanford ProNet or MIT

ProNet. Alumni register by filling out a diskette supplied by their alumni association. The diskette contains a program that walks the registrant through an extensive history of education, work background, and skills base. The information collected on the standardized profile form is far more detailed than a traditional resume—a typical profile is six pages long.

To request information, alumni can call the following telephone numbers:

Cal ProNet (UC/Berkeley)	(510) 845-9879
Caltech ProNet (Calif. Inst. Tech.)	(818) 356-0654
Carnegie-Mellon ProNet (Carnegie-Mellon Univ.)	(412) 687-5011
Columbia University	(212) 870-2530
Cornell University	(607) 255-2390
Illinois ProNet (Univ. of Illinois)	(217) 333-1471
Michigan ProNet (Univ. of Michigan)	(313) 741-7220
MIT ProNet (Mass. Inst. of Technology)	(617) 248-5899
Ohio State ProNet (Ohio State Univ.)	(614) 291-6486
Stanford ProNet (Stanford Univ.)	(415) 691-1600
Texas ProNet (Univ. of Texas/Austin)	(512) 472-0526
UCLA ProNet (UCLA)	(310) 824-0059
University of Chicago	(312) 702-2150
Yale ProNet (Yale Univ.)	(203) 432-7871

If for any reason you must contact the service directly, use the address given above.

How Long Is a Resume Retained?

If you update it annually, the resume remains in the database throughout your lifetime.

How Do You Know if the Database Is Working for You?

You can tell by the quality of the positions, the accuracy of the matches, and the frequency of the contacts you experience.

How Do You Revise Your Resume?

Each individual keeps a copy of his or her diskette, which can be used to revise a resume. Updating is done at no charge.

Other Facts

Started in 1987, University ProNet is the only database for university alumni operated by member institutions—it is not a third-party vendor. University ProNet does not work with executive search firms but only with employers and only on specific types of open positions. Individuals can block the release of their resumes to any number of companies.

3

New: In-House Applicant Tracking Systems

Smart Software Is Changing the Way Hiring Happens in America—Here's What You Must Know

In the last chapter, we looked at **external** resume database services—services that inventory people.

In this chapter, we examine another way to inventory people—the new **internal** systems companies are using to electronically process their own pool of applicants whose unsolicited resumes come in "over the transom."

Today's front-running companies may use an external system, an internal system, or a combination of both.

Tracking systems are not exclusively for employers. Executive recruiters, who (for a fee) help client organizations find and appraise candidates for specific positions, also track applicants with these systems.

"We'll keep your resume on file." How many times have you heard that one?

The artfully constructed resume you pieced together dream by dream, tactic by tactic, and word by word is handed over to a corporate recruiter who, for all you know, orbits it into space. You never hear another word about it.

You've tried every trick in several books, from sending your resume to the company president claiming you both are alumni of the same university, to changing your status from job seeker to shareholder by buying one share of stock and asking the director of investor relations to pass your resume along.

Nothing is working, and the absence of a response is dashing your hopes and dreams. It happens time after time: the waiting, the anticipating. You begin to feel discouraged, frustrated, disheartened, rejected, depressed. What happened to those hundreds of resumes you sent? Doesn't anyone care? Why long-time-no-hear—from anyone?

A wall of silence is one of the real gut-wrenching complaints job seekers make about human resource specialists and hiring managers. You wonder: Why don't they have the common courtesy to acknowledge the receipt of your resume? Don't they remember what it was like when they were on the outside looking in?

You're not alone in having a pity party. Being ignored hurts. The discomfort you feel from being disregarded is largely because a resume mirrors *you*—it is a kind of proof of your individual existence, an edited portion of your life story. None of us actually expects to get a job offer from each and every employer to whom a resume is submitted, but we certainly expect acknowledgment that we exist.

Beyond mere wounded feelings, the underlying reason acknowledgment letters are so important is that high morale during a job search is essential to your success. Essential! When you are hammered by rejection—which is how you may subconsciously interpret the silent treatment—your sense of self-value begins to slip and you unknowingly broadcast messages of desperation: SOS . . . SOS.

Employers can smell despondency a mile away and will go to China and back to avoid it. Most managers try to be admirable people, but it's not their job to hire pitiful people with low self-esteem for whom they feel sorry. It's their job to hire winners.

The linkage of acknowledgment letters to the success of your job hunt is subtle, even obscure—and very real.

Why don't companies know this and get back to you promptly? The short answer is: staggering workloads.

Switch viewpoints, if you will, to the other side of the recruitment desk. Pity the poor beleaguered corporate recruiter who is told to find the best person for the job—fast!

No R.S.V.P.? Here's Why.

It's an old complaint from demoralized job hunters who have sent resumes in response to a recruitment ad:

"I am frustrated and disappointed by the insensitivity of human resource people. About half of the time, I hear nothing at all. Even when I do, the response is anything but prompt. It took one firm I applied to eight weeks to send me a rejection letter and another firm six weeks to tell me that they were not planning to fill the position after all. A third firm I've sent resumes to has failed to get back to me after five weeks."

It's sad but true: no one has your sense of urgency in your job hunt. This explains part of the time lag that seems an eternity when you're on the waiting end. Beyond that, is it really accurate to make a human resource person the villain of the piece?

Management experts say no, that it's scapegoating to lay the blame of no response or a slow response at the feet of human resource staff. The HR specialist is merely the focal point of the transaction and can act only when the hiring manager (or selection committee) makes a decision on the timing of the interviews. Unfortunately for job seekers, a hiring manager's attention to the employment process is not always a high priority.

Further delays arise when the work situation changes. Internal candidates may suddenly become available, budget problems may require a rethinking of hiring plans, a planned product introduction may be canceled, the word may get around that the company is being sold or relocated—any number of revised conditions can overnight alter the hiring process.

Not getting a response is even more likely when you send an unsolicited resume. Yes, a lack of acknowledgment is rude, but it's a fact of life in busy offices. Smart software systems can—and, we hope, will—change this part of the hiring process for the better.

As the recruiter stares at a room crowded with filing cabinets, which in turn are stuffed with paper resumes, a vague memory surfaces of a great resume of the perfect applicant. "Now let's see . . . where is it?" Fifteen minutes later, no luck. The recruiter clearly remembers only that the perfect applicant's resume is filed away somewhere. Finding it will take forever and usually does.

The search may disintegrate as the recruiter tries to negotiate a landfill of paper. "Potential candidates who are highly qualified may be overlooked because their resume is misfiled—or lost on another hiring manager's desk," explains a corporate vice president of human resources who has looked for many needles in thousands of paper stacks.

Another human resource manager says finding the best employee for a job can be a dizzying, time-consuming, expensive process. "We used to have six people standing at copy machines all day," she explains. That was before her company found relief in electronic recruitment technology.

Because a mountain of paper can be a migraine to manage, leading-edge companies are turning to a raft of new software muscle programs to drive high-tech recruitment systems. They're doing it for the same reasons the Clinton Administration used an automated process to help fill 3,000 to 4,000 political jobs.

There was political input too, but the workhorse of the Clinton employment effort was an *internal, computerized applicant tracking system.*

Without automation, cascading waves of an estimated 100,000 resumes figuratively would have swept volunteers on the Clinton team into the Potomac River. The tide of resumes simply could not have been managed by manual systems.

Job seekers represented a wide assortment of talents, ranging from sophisticated molecular scientists to a mother who was willing to take any job and, to prove it, enclosed a picture of her daughter dressed for Halloween as a Clinton campaign bus.

EXECUTIVE RECRUITERS FACE SAME PAPER MOUNTAINS

Executive search consultants, sometimes called executive recruiters or technical recruiters, decided in the 1970s that they'd had enough of paper farming. Once they had seen the joys of automation, they never looked back.

Executive search consultants are the hired hunters who stalk the best and brightest managerial and professional troops in the nation. Also called by the pejorative and informal title of "headhunters," these talent seekers began to develop computer-driven resume databases and applicant tracking systems two decades ago. At first, the systems were on the primitive side. Today, the systems used by many of the search firms are as advanced as those in use at leading corporations. Other systems remain unsophisticated. It's a mixed bag.

If you're hoping to catch a recruiter's eye and be singled out from the crowd of hopefuls who want bigger and better jobs, pay close attention to this chapter and to our companion book, *Electronic Resume Revolution.*

A search consultant literally searches outward, gathering leads from many sources. But contemporary executive search firms maintain internal applicant tracking systems alongside their subscriptions to electronic resume databases of candidates, compiled from various sources.

When a likely name turns up, the search consultants are soon on the telephone checking out the lead.

When you want a recruiter to discover you, to tap you on the shoulder with a sword and raise you to the heights of corporate nobility, get into as many databases as possible. This includes those of professional societies, trade associations, and college alumni. A companion smart move is to get into as many recruiters' applicant tracking systems as possible.

To identify search consultants, check the annual *Directory of Executive Recruiters* (Kennedy and Kennedy, Inc., Fitzwilliam, NH).

APPLICANT TRACKING SYSTEMS EASE PAPER OVERLOAD

Whether business or politics was the cause, organizations that hire people have awakened to a new realization: They somehow must change the way work gets done if they are to meet the goal of achieving more productivity and profit with fewer people and costs. They must change—or they won't survive.

If you've been active in the job market recently, you know that, for many organizations, the decade of the 1990s has been one of stress and struggle.

When employers find out they can use applicant tracking systems, artificial intelligence, expert systems, total recall approaches, and scanning with optical character recognition to significantly reduce costs and improve the quality and efficiency of their employment function, they're saying, "Let's do it."

And the word is getting out fast. Simply put, to make the employment situation manageable, internal applicant tracking systems have become an integral part of the way large corporations—and, increasingly, midsize companies—do business.

What about companies that are too small to have their own internal systems? They are starting to buy time on systems operated by commercial firms, the applicant tracking service bureaus.

Whether an employer is filling jobs from external independent resume databases or from an internal applicant tracking system, the implications for you, the job seeker or career self-manager, are enormous.

There's no doubt about it: The new intelligent software technology sweeping America has both a dramatic upside and a troubling downside.

RESUME AUTOMATION: THE UPSIDE

Communication

For those times when you do not receive an immediate job offer, resume software technology certainly is better mannered than traditional manual processing systems. It permits human resource specialists, with very little effort, to let you know your resume made it to their desks.

Most applicant tracking systems, with the click of a mouse or the stroke of a key, can generate a letter saying "We'll keep your resume on file." But these employment managers are not merely banging a kettledrum of little white lies.

They mean it because computers have made resume databases possible; they are a form of new human resource wealth.

Once a nuisance, resumes are now warmly welcomed because every hire from a company's own resume bank is one less expense to farm out to employment services or recruitment advertising. It's like saving money by eating in rather than dining out.

Inclusion

There is another benefit to having a computer read your resume. The machine can provide the break you need to get into the running. When the economy thunders down too many resumes on a human resource department, a normally good system can be reduced to a 90-pound weakling.

Instead of a screening by an experienced employment manager, the initial resume task may be a sorting dumped on untrained clerical workers.

Typically, these inexperienced aides are told to sort in three stacks: "yes" for a current opening, "future possibles" for a later one, and "no interest" for those documents that will be unceremoniously snuffed.

If the clerical screener doesn't understand what your resume says—and finds some technical resumes are as mystifying as the Dead Sea Scrolls—you're history. Worse, if the clerical screener happens to harbor a bias that works against you, your resume is dead on arrival.

Fairness

By contrast, the argument can be made that the early winnowing process is more meticulous—and fairer—when performed by computer reasoning than by humans.

Computers, even when guided by expert systems and artificial intelligence, don't move away from their "factory installed" overall guidelines. Humans, shaped by differing life experiences, may unknowingly screen with bias or ignorance.

Bias can enter the picture at any stage of human intervention, but if a computer is on the job, you'll probably get past its electronic sentry and into the database. Once in, you'll have a chance of being pulled out for hiring consideration.

Returning to the issue of fairness, companies have a practical reason to support objective recruitment and promotion policies: Employers that discriminate are sitting ducks for legal nightmares and severe financial penalties.

"The very nature of resume automated systems enhances evenhandedness," says an employment manager whose department has been using an applicant tracking system for more than a year. "Most programs produce a list of all appropriate candidates in ranked order, based on the predetermined values assigned to job skills," he adds.

"Systems can be used to electronically store resumes that have been 'sanitized' of any inappropriate information, such as age, gender, race, and disability," he explains.

(After hiring takes place, the data removed by sanitizing can be reshuffled electronically to instantly produce mandated equal employment opportunity and affirmative action reports for companies holding federal contracts.)

Multi-Opportunities

Another positive note for resume software technology is that once inside it, your resume automatically casts a wider net.

By the use of keywords, you are considered for every job opening within striking distance of your abilities.

When you are preparing a paper resume, you may choose to place early in the document a summary of your qualifications. Depending on the circumstances, it's often advisable to lead off with a fairly well-defined objective so that resume readers will know to which occupational tribe you belong.

Employers have a habit of speed reading and can skim a resume in ten seconds flat. By eliminating the guesswork of how you would fit into an organization, you position yourself to be chosen.

With computers, an employer is not forced to wade through your resume trying to decide whether your qualifications will wrap around the job's requirements or essential functions. These well-oiled hiring machines may find your name in any of several categories, rather than in just one.

You may, for instance, jump to the recruiter's screen as a candidate for *mechanical engineer,* or *manager with five years' experience,* or *quality control specialist.* Maybe you'll even turn up in the *technical writing* category as well.

Now suppose you're an A-1 mechanical engineer and you wrote the book on quality control, but you have only two years' managerial experience and writing isn't your strong point.

In a search with the descriptors given above, your name may surface and you'll make the first cut. But you probably will fade away if the database is rich with better qualified candidates.

(There are no guarantees in electronic hide-and-seek. It's like a poker game: You don't know what cards the other players are holding.)

You're an intelligent person—you know that no one will hire you as a technical writer. What's more, you lack more than half the requested managerial experience. So what good does it do, you ask, to make the first cut?

The benefit of being nominated—of being yanked out of electronic oblivion—is that you have a fighting chance to wind up in someone's office for an interview. Getting inside is always better than being locked outside. It's that simple.

Employers don't always know exactly what they want when they write job requisitions. They may ask for ten "requirements" and, depending on the pool of applicants, settle for someone they like who has only seven of the requirements, particularly when compensatory strengths can be plugged into the gaps.

Speed

An advantage of applicant tracking systems is the speeded-up timetable they make possible. Before the 1980s, an employment manager shopping for the most qualified members of the available work force might have used a manual system no more sophisticated than graphpaper chart comparisons of candidates' qualifications.

Down the left side of the sheet were the candidates' names. Along the top of the page were specifications of the job. Checkmarks or numerical rankings were jotted down after each candidate's name.

The employment manager and the hiring manager sometimes met and reviewed the listing, often many pages long. They selected the most promising candidates and studied their resumes, cover letters, letters of reference, and other material, trying to rank the applicants in a descending order of most qualified to least qualified.

An employment manager for a major brewery that receives 40,000 job applications a year says, "After half an hour of juggling applications and trying to keep 10 or 15 candidates' information in mind, the managers' brain may be in a morass."

Now that resumes can be scanned and automatically sorted and ranked (by preprogrammed values for each job specification), the process is almost as simple and fast as 1–2–3, *click!* We call the process "resume surfing" because it's designed to catch the best waves of candidates. Resume surfing takes about 1.5 seconds per page, and ranking doesn't take much longer. Making faster decisions about whom to interview hurries the hiring process along.

Understanding the String-Along Game

Despite the fast start that smart software gives to the employment process, speedy hiring isn't always the outcome. Why do job seekers experience interminable waiting for a firm offer to come through, even when employment or hiring managers have indicated interest?

Sometimes, the answer is simple: They hate to say no. At other times, the answer is complex: It could be any of a million reasons. So the managers stall and string you along:

"We want to hire you, but we have to get the paperwork from the regional office."

"We need to see a few more people before we can do the deal, but personally I'm pulling for you."

"We're having a great quarter. When a business pickup is solid, the hiring freeze should end."

Some string-alongs actually are true. So what? The end result for you is still zero.

Among signs that a string-along has some degree of truth: Your references may be contacted, or a hiring manager may put a time frame on the conversation, "If you don't hear from HR this week, call me."

Still, these signs are not a paycheck. Even after a verbal offer, the situation can fall apart, leaving you with a loss of job and a lack of momentum. The lesson to be learned is that you, as a prudent person, must continue your all-out job hunt until the day you report to work.

Technology may not hurry the hiring decision along. The action steps are in the human realm of control, and you know what that means. The actual choice of a candidate and the start date for a new hire may drag out for reasons quite beyond the scope of computers.

Bull's-Eye Matching

Another plus for resume automation is that you need not, ever again, hear that unpopular "O" word. Being told repeatedly that you are "overqualified" for a position may be true, but it's also a synonym for age discrimination.

If a job really is below your capabilities, you shouldn't be interviewing for it. The computer won't let you be called in only to suffer one more rejection in a personal interview.

The flip side is that if you really want the job and you are willing to take steps backward to get it, you won't be given the chance to persuasively plead your case. You may not have to hear the "O" word, but you may have to read it in a regret letter that describes how your skills overshoot the position.

Other boons of computer-driven applicant tracking may become apparent as the systems grow, but one other point jumps out: It's time to take a new look at broadcast letters.

Makes Cold-Calling Cost-Effective

Broadcast letter writing is cold-calling by mail. You compile a list of companies and organizations that could hire you for the kind of work you want, and you send out a mass mailing of your resume with a cover letter.

Many career specialists are lukewarm on this strategy. They believe it is costly and ineffective to mass mail to a large universe of employers without very careful preparation and selection.

Now that applicant tracking systems encourage electronic storage of resumes, sometimes for years or a lifetime, mailing even a few resumes may be well worth your time and postage. As a practical matter, well-done broadcast mailing is no longer a one-time shot, but a kind of investment in your career.

Helps Laid-Off Workers

It's rough out there. In the early 1980s, 90 percent of dismissed workers found similar work; in the 1990s, only about 25 percent have been so fortunate.

Some lucky technical personnel who are losing their jobs are getting a helping hand from a spin-off of applicant tracking systems. The technology, in this incarnation, is a computerized integrated staffing system known as the Technical Available Personnel (TAP) network. It opened for business in late 1992.

The TAP network uses the applicant tracking system marketed by Resumix to inventory resumes from companies that are downsizing and make those resumes available to companies that are hiring.

Outplaced job seekers pay no more than $20 per year, often less. Corporate members of the TAP consortium, chiefly high-tech defense contractors, pick up most of the tab. In some cases, government agencies pitch in to pay the resume processing fee.

The TAP network—and other networks that can be expected to imitate it—is a welcome recognition by corporate giants that good workers are not disposable people but a valuable national resource to be recycled with care, compassion, and common sense.

Even with everything they have going for them, applicant tracking systems—particularly the "plug-and-chuggers" in which rigid requirements are plugged into systems that chug away without human intervention until they fetch the desired short list of candidates—have a few decided drawbacks.

RESUME AUTOMATION: THE DOWNSIDE

The biggest problems intelligent software systems create for job seekers are described here.

Excludes All but Top Picks

The systems skim the cream off the crop of applicants, taking the best and leaving the rest. That's okay if you're at the top of the list.

If you're not, you must find ways to get around the system, such as human networking—using all your personal contacts to get fair consideration.

Machine Error

Scanning equipment can malfunction or misread your document, leaving your resume out in left field. You can't do much about this. But if you never seem to be among the chosen, it's worth reviewing your resume to be sure it's clean copy that isn't giving scanners and optical character recognition software fits.

What Happens When You Apply Three Times to the Same Company?

One area of job search that is ripe for rethinking is the practice of submitting multiple resumes and cover letters to the same employer, especially resumes that are customized to fit a particular position.

The old advice still holds for companies that use manual systems: Tailor your approach for each position. Try to match your qualifications point-by-point with the specifications of the position.

In the accounting field, for instance, you might emphasize your international auditing experience for a position with responsibilities beyond U.S. borders, but, two months later, remake your resume for the same employer to focus on your electronic data processing auditing skills. Still later, you may see that the same company is advertising a position for an accountant with internal auditing experience. You have that too, so you rush back to your word processor and print out a third resume that headlines your internal auditing experience. All three resumes are true; each reflects a facet of your background, depending on the job opening. You have engaged in situational resume writing, tilting each resume toward the target job opening.

For processing in sizable manual systems, situational resume writing is good strategy. The chances are slim that all three documents will turn up on the same desk, particularly if they are submitted over a period of months.

By contrast, for processing in electronic systems, situational resume writing may or may not be good strategy. Here's why.

When your resume is scanned into a company's database, theoretically you are considered each time an electronic search ferrets out appropriate candidates. Supposedly, you need not reapply for each new opening in which you're interested. The computer should poke around and find out that your qualifications are relevant when you are a potentially good match for a job opening.

But because of the possibility, however remote, that scanning equipment will misread, miscode, or even eat your resume, it's probably a good idea to resubmit a resume to the same company for each job you want.

When you customize your resume for each opening (situational resume writing), the issue becomes iffy. The idea is similar to saying more or less the same thing to each person in serial interviews—perhaps six people from the same company may interview you at separate times. You must come across as the same person in all of your resumes that reside in the same internal database.

This is particularly important when dealing with executive recruiters, most of whom have databases.

Again, assuming a trio of resumes, try to emerge as the same person on each document. Chances are very high that the computer will flag all three resumes, making it easy for a screener to compare them. The screener may think, "First this woman said her strong suit was international auditing. Next she says she's a whiz at EDP auditing. Then she positions herself as an internal auditor. Sounds like resume inflation to me."

If you submit multiple resumes, take pains not to be seen as an individual who plays games with your qualifications.

We're in favor of multiple resumes and situational resume writing—as long as the truth isn't stretched to the point of misrepresentation. Sending new paper each time you apply for different positions at the same company is wise. Just as computers are not infallible, human resume screeners may misjudge or lose your resume, or there may be new people, or the job requirements may change.

Even if a trio of your resumes does turn up on the screen or in the same file folder, it probably won't hurt your chances or project you as being desperate for employment. An equally likely supposition is that you're really interested in the company and deserve to be interviewed.

With good reason, most job hunt guides urge you to do advance research on where you want to work. The more you know about a prospective employer, the more easily you can show how your credentials match a position's requirements.

In this new era of electronic job search, add one more item to your research list: Has the company yet switched to an internal applicant tracking system?

If so, keep records and make sure all your resumes are written on the same music sheet even though the lyrics are different.

Salary Buster

Perhaps the most distressing problem is that some automated resume systems sharply reduce your salary negotiating power.

The salary issue is a constant problem, for a number of reasons. None of them is easy to solve. When electronic recruitment technology meets the salary issue, the problem gets worse. Here's what we mean.

If you have been reading job hunt guides, you know:

1. *It is in your best interests* not *to discuss salary until a job offer has been made.* Once you know a company wants you, the negotiation is between parties with virtually equal power. Until a job offer comes, the employer is calling the shots and is in total control. The employer owns all the uniforms, bats, and balls, and you're not even on first base.
2. *Until you talk through the position, you don't know what the work is worth.* You need to know the job's details. If you agree to a price prematurely, you're buying, with your labor, into a new ball game you know very little about—not a good move.

These are two good reasons why it's an error to state on your resume either your salary history or the salary you expect. You probably know what pay you'd like to have or what you need to pay the bills, but that isn't necessarily your market value.

Research to find out what you're worth in the job market, and fight hard to get it. Even if you've been underpaid for a while, this is difficult but manageable. Several books discuss this topic in adequate detail, such as Jack Chapman's *How To Make $1000 a Minute Negotiating Your Salaries and Raises* (Ten Speed Press, 1988).

Your original resume or a standardized form may have no salary information, but you may still be asked to supply salary history or expectations on a supplemental form. This is not to your advantage, but there's little you can do other than comply.

View a call for salary history or expectations not as a request but as a command. When a computer is told to pull names of applicants—say, managers in the $40,000 to $50,000 bracket—it won't find you if you have ducked the issue by writing "Will discuss" in the space where you're asked about money.

(The "Will discuss" answer often works fine in human reviews of applicants, but not well at all when computers read your application.)

Another salary buster occurs when your salary identity dwells in a database over a period of years and becomes out-of-date. You will have grown professionally and will be qualified to earn more money, but a resume lodged in an in-house system won't reflect that fact unless you remember to send in an updated resume.

You probably have some reservations about having your personal financial data float around where any employee with a password can spy it out. According to makers of applicant tracking systems, access to confidential data and specific functions is restricted to authorized users. True? Untrue?

Here's one job-seeking manager's opinion: "I may be unduly cynical but I read the same news stories about computer hackers breaking into CIA computers that you do."

The privacy issue remains to be proven employer-by-employer, but the plain truth is that electronic resume databases are here to stay. Let's see how a representative in-house system actually functions in a company.

HOW AN APPLICANT TRACKING SYSTEM WORKS

Each of the major internal applicant tracking systems offers varying performance features.

Some offer blow-you-away sophistication and virtuosity in preparing every human resource report a company could possibly want. Others are less ambitious. All of them provide similar functions in a new recruiting frontier.

These are the journey legs as your resume voyages through a database.

Scanning

Your original resume—the one you labored at writing, or paid dearly to have written—is welcomed into the applicant tracking system's database by the amazing scanning and optical character recognition technology mentioned earlier. The technology reads and absorbs its contents, adding your resume to a huge computerized pool of job talent.

Your credentials may be sorted and stored in a number of ways, including alphabetically, regionally, or by specialty skills. An example is given in Figure 3–1.

Dating

The software automatically stamps the date on your records, which will later show when your resume was received and entered.

Being polite as well as smart, the software now says, "It's time to confirm that we received this applicant's resume," and an acknowledgment letter goes out. It too is date-stamped.

Requisition Tracking

The hiring manager issues (through the human resource department) a job requisition to the system. Upon receipt of the requisition,

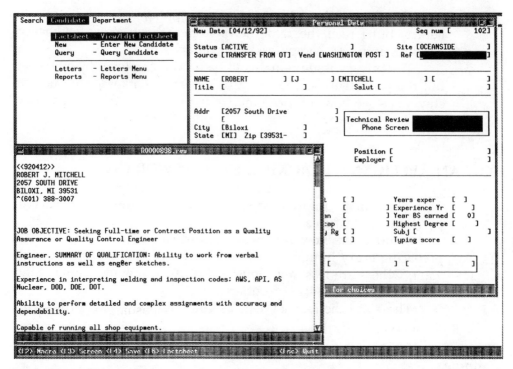

Figure 3–1   Computer Screen Produced by Applicant Tracking System. (Courtesy of SmartSearch2/Advanced Personnel Systems, Inc., Oceanside, CA)

the system switches over to a "requisition tracking" mode—and is off and running on an electronic sprint to find "best match" candidates.

Most tracking systems have predefined categories, such as education and industry experience. They are accessed automatically.

The hiring manager can ask for other categories specific to the position, such as the ability to use a specific brand of graphic-design software or to analyze toxic air samples. By inserting keywords, the search can be tailored to a gnat's eyebrow. The process is called "building a search." It means matching the exact specifications of a job requisition with the credentials of applicants in the database.

Weighting Keywords

The hiring manager, through the use of a sliding scale, can weight each predefined category or tailored keyword according to its level of importance.

For example, the descriptors used in the search may call for an "engineering technician" who has a two-year "associate degree," but may give preference to an "engineering technologist" who holds a four-year "bachelor's degree." The technician must either live in or be willing to move to "St. Louis, MO." The information from the categories will be "matched" with any and all resumes in the system that fit the job requisition.

In this overview, let's assume your resume fits the job requisition and is still in the running. The tracking system has zeroed in on the following matching keywords in your resume:

▶ *Personal data*—your name, address, home and work telephone numbers, planning data for equal employment opportunity and affirmative action policies, residence status, and willingness to relocate and travel.

▶ *Skills data*—your skills and related proficiencies.

▶ *Education data*—schools you attended (and the dates), field of study, degrees and certificates earned, licenses and permits held, and professional association memberships.

▶ *Prior experience*—your previous employers, usually with the present or last being placed first; position titles, salaries, and duties.

▶ *Employment testing*—job test dates and results (the system can track these).

▶ *Applicant contact*—records of all communications and contacts with you, from initial acknowledgment of your resume's receipt to interview schedules or acceptance/regret letters.

Ranking

If you're tapped electronically to become a "screen star," the software will, within seconds, add your candidacy to others similarly qualified and present you within a ranked list.

In many cases, the human resource specialist or hiring manager views your original resume, along with the capsule of data pulled out from the resume (called an applicant summary or an extracted summary), on a computer monitor.

In some systems, your information is stored in an online database in three versions:

1. A capsule of name, rank, serial number, and categories into which you fit;

2. An applicant summary from the original resume, or a standardized form (it makes comparisons easier);

3. An exact image of your resume.

The data in any or all versions are instantly available to a resume reader.

Even in less complex tracking systems, the resume reader can select an individual name on the computer screen's matching display and bring up the entire resume. Usually, these tracking systems will highlight (electronically illuminate) on the screen the precise specifications that qualify the resume for the requisition. This feature gives the searcher an instant grasp of how each candidate matches the job requisition, and makes it easy to see how, "on screen" at least, you fit the job.

Qualified candidates are listed according to how each person matches the requisition. The best matches appear at the top of the computer screen; the fewest matches are at the bottom.

The relative score of each candidate appears as a number next to the candidate's name on the ranked list. As an example, those with "bachelor degree" will be listed ahead of those with "associate degree" if that's what the search dictates.

In the earlier search for an engineering technologist willing to move to St. Louis, resumes from that city will be listed ahead of other geographic locations, providing all other categories are equal.

Publishing

The electronic genie can be told to conjure up any or all of the information about you and your competitors in hard (print) copy, faxes, or e-mail.

In a flash, the searcher can send the selected resumes to be run out on laser printers or by fax to hiring managers across the hall or across the nation. Let's hope you're among the favored.

Cross-Searching

In a slightly different scenario, your name may not come up as the result of a newly ordered job requisition search, but as a possible answer to some unfinished business.

Not infrequently, a department manager spends months searching high and low for the perfect candidate for a hard-to-fill position. The manager has left a standing order to call when/if the perfect person comes along. Let's assume you're that perfect person. When your resume is scanned into the system, a flare goes up, alerting the manager that the human resource department may have struck pay dirt.

As you can see, the possibilities of a resume tracking system are vast and potentially rewarding for your job search. But when you get a warm and friendly customized letter acknowledging your resume, don't get too confident just yet. The signature on your letter really wasn't handwritten. It was generated automatically from the system's image memory of personalized signatures. Amazing, these machines.

TOMORROW'S CUTTING-EDGE TECHNOLOGY TODAY

For the human resource specialist or employment manager reading this book, this section gives a brief overview of the many commercial products that can make your job easier.

For the job seeker reading this book, the remainder of this chapter may or may not be of primary interest. We recommend that you read it because it gives clues about some of the newest software programs designed specifically to handle the huge amounts of resume processing and applicant tracking information. It generally is useful to know the conditions under which the person on the human resource side of the desk is working. However, if you're pressed for time, skip to Chapter 4.

Constantly aware of keen competition and a thirst for even more applications, software companies continue to upgrade and innovate their programming. To remain competitive in a rapidly growing market of employers, innovation is urgent.

Putting the electronic recruitment issue into perspective, a director of corporate human services management recently said management demands swift solutions in today's market, and the question for employment managers in the 1990s isn't "to scan or not to scan," but rather "to compete or not to compete." In the not too distant future, it will be normal practice in American industry for resumes to be read by computer.

(For the job seeker in the 1990s, perhaps the question isn't "to learn computer job search or not to learn computer job search," but rather "to compete or not to compete.")

We have identified more than a dozen applicant tracking software systems currently being used by corporate America. More companies appear yearly. Nearly all of these applicant tracking systems basically work the same way, but each has at least one or two distinctions, a few of which are substantial.

Most applicant tracking systems process resume information by digesting the entire contents of the document. However, some copy the exact image of the resume being scanned and some don't. Although the first approach takes up a lot more computer memory, some human resource managers say having an exact copy of an applicant's resume on their screen can be helpful with judging the following criteria:

▶ *The way an applicant lays out a resume.* The hiring specialist or manager may want an advance look at the applicant's organizational qualities and neatness. How carefully designed and complete is the original resume?

▶ *The way an applicant spells and uses grammar.* This speaks for itself.

▶ *An applicant's use of a professional resume service.* Some human resource specialists abhor professionally prepared resumes because they look as though they rolled off an assembly line and often are so overproduced that they project Madison Avenue puffery. Human resource specialists may wonder why the applicant needs such heavy packaging if he or she is such hot stuff. Still other hiring specialists and managers couldn't care less who prepared the resume.

There is another advantage in having the exact copy of the resume in the database: Some factual detail on the resume may not be captured by applicant tracking systems that rearrange the resume into a standardized format.

An applicant may list information that gives an interviewer some insight into his or her personality—for example, something signifying risk taking, such as "skydiving" as a hobby—but that information probably would never be known if the actual resume were not retrieved for viewing.

The overall goals of any applicant tracking system are to be fast, consistent, and thorough, and to give every job seeker the same treatment.

Applicant tracking software can provide employers with unbiased candidate evaluation procedures and with effective, detailed record-keeping systems. For example, an applicant tracking program can make it much easier to document compliance with government employment requirements, when necessary.

A spokesperson for Bell Atlantic, a 73,000-plus employee corporation with a number of subsidiaries nationwide, says her office receives an average of 75,000 to 100,000 unsolicited resumes a year.

"We're trying to hold that number down, but it tends to go up and down with the economy," says the spokesperson. "We attempt to limit our unsolicited resumes from applicants not likely to be good matches through using an 800 number that details company requirements."

Bell Atlantic hires more than 500 professional and technical personnel annually, and another 5,000 to 6,000 nonexempt employees, including temporary and part-time workers.

"We used to hire a lot of college graduates right out of school, but we're hiring more seasoned veterans now than we used to," she says. "We formerly hired a lot of entry-level workers so that we could train them internally, but now we look for more experienced, job specific knowledge, people who can 'hit the ground running.'"

She explains that her company utilizes three types of scanning and imaging: (1) image character recognition, (2) intelligent character recognition, and (3) optical mark recognition.

Job seekers applying for nonexempt positions at Bell Atlantic usually do not submit a resume. Instead, they fill out an application, which is scanned with an intelligent character recognition system that converts the handwritten application into a basic resume, according to the spokesperson.

The applicant tracking system then handles this basic resume much like it would handle submitted resumes, only on a different level of hiring requirements.

As for all other job seekers submitting resumes, the spokesperson says Bell Atlantic no longer keeps the paper once the resume has been scanned into the company's database in Arlington, Virginia.

"That was a big step forward in gaining valuable filing space," says the spokesperson. "It's [the applicant tracking system] not only reduced the working space we need, but we've significantly reduced the staff we used to need in the human resources department." She adds that being able to operate in less space amounts to a significant savings because of the high price tag on office space in the major metropolitan areas where the company operates.

Bell Atlantic has taken the art of electronic applicant tracking even further. It has developed a system that interacts with Resumix and allows any employee of the telecommunications company to access a special 800 telephone number to inquire what jobs are available within the company.

"You need your social security number and a special company PIN [personal identification number] in order to access the system," explains the spokesperson. "This is to keep independent recruiters from getting into the system to take advantage. This program is strictly for our employees."

Once the system is accessed via a push-button telephone, she notes, the employee can either apply right on the phone for the job desired, or request a more detailed job description for the opening.

"We fax the job description directly to the employee. Most workers have access to a company fax," she observes. "Faxing is less

So Much for Australia . . .

After being laid off from his defense industry job at Northrop Corporation in the Los Angeles area, computer whiz James Blanton figured the timing was right for him to see a bit of the world. Why not work his way around the globe? Why not start in Australia? Blanton began searching for an Australian employer who needed his skills.

"I bought this job search book listing foreign employment opportunities and there were a lot of listings for Australian companies," says Blanton. "A friend of mine was helping me mail out applications. I asked her to send my resume to all the companies listed for Australia."

Two weeks later, Blanton says, he received a call from San Francisco-based Bank of America. Unaware of exactly who had been sent his resume, Blanton quickly found out that among the companies listed for Australian opportunities was Bank of America.

"I guess they have some sort of operation there," he says. "Anyway, when they called, we scheduled a meeting. I was offered a job about a week after the interview."

Blanton accepted a systems engineering position in computer security—not in Australia, but at Bank of America's Concord (California) Technical Center, just east of Oakland, California.

What happened was this: Blanton's mailed resume had been received and placed into the company's computerized applicant tracking system, which quickly tagged it as matching the requirements for one of the bank's technical openings.

Blanton says he isn't aware of what sort of system the human resource department uses, but he sure is pleased with its results.

"I couldn't be happier with the way things worked out," says Blanton.

And Australia?

"Well, I have a pen pal in New Zealand who gave me the idea of going down under in the first place, but that's on the back burner now," Blanton says as he glances appreciatively at a picture of the Golden Gate Bridge on his wall.

expensive than using either internal mail or the U.S. mail system, according to an internal study."

She says that, during a typical week, 6,000 to 8,000 employee calls come into the in-house job openings system. In turn, about 1,000 faxes are sent, detailing anywhere from 200 to 400 positions that are open.

"We hire inside among our existing employees whenever possible," the Bell Atlantic spokesperson explains.

She adds that nonexempt employees (workers who legally must be paid at overtime rates for overtime work) can arrange for a standing application (the application remains in place until an advertised position is filled). This ensures that the interested employee is considered for that job without needing to call every day or every week to check on its status.

San Francisco-based Bank of America, California's largest and one of the nation's biggest financial institutions, uses a major applicant tracking system, which officials at the bank prefer not to name. A spokesperson for Bank of America's Systems Engineering Group in San Francisco has a staff of ten human resource specialists and recruiters to service the division.

"This applicant tracking system allows us to become our own personnel agency," the spokesperson explains. "We get our resumes and applications from a variety of sources: media advertising, career fairs, internal transfers, and computer networks."

The Systems Engineering Group spokesperson says his division, which has more than 4,000 workers, receives an average of 150 resumes weekly. "It can be as high as 400 to 500 a week, depending upon how many ads we've run in the media," he adds.

"We put resumes in file folders before going to this system four years ago," the spokesperson recalls. He says automated tracking has proven itself. "We're committed to the applicant tracking system. And the other divisions are watching our progress closely and with great interest."

The Systems Engineering Group generally hires between 350 to 400 people per year. "That includes the transfers from within our employee ranks," explains the spokesperson. He says the applicant tracking system has allowed more efficiency in his department.

"We've not only downsized in personnel, but where our old manual way would require five recruiters to handle 150 [position] openings, today three recruiters handle 200 openings," he notes. "We certainly can do a much higher volume of work with fewer people because of this system."

The spokesperson finds it fascinating that a computerized applicant tracking system allows the first two or three steps of the job hiring process to be accomplished "automatically" without human assistance.

"One thing it [the system] can't do, though, is speak directly to the candidate to get an even closer match for the final hiring," he concludes. "You can't take the human factor out of this."

PRC, Inc., of McLean, Virginia, a professional services company that does 75 percent of its business with the federal government, uses Resumix as its human resource applicant tracking system. An employment manager for PRC says his company has more than 25,000 resumes scanned into the database. The 7,500-employee corporation has used Resumix since early 1991.

"We receive about 20,000 resumes yearly," says the manager, who was with the company before it installed Resumix. "It's a real time-saver. The number of work hours we've saved is significant."

The manager says until he was appointed to head his department's applicant tracking process, no one really had a handle on just how much time was saved.

His department has about 15 human resource specialists who use Resumix daily to handle the many job requisitions that come from PRC managers monthly.

"This type of programming is really in its infancy," the manager explains. "It is very important to implement the system properly to take advantage of all its capabilities. Resumix's programming, I think, is state-of-the-art."

A SAMPLING OF APPLICANT TRACKING SYSTEMS

▶ *AbraTrak:* Abra Cadabra Human Resource Software, 888 Executive Center Drive, Suite 300, St. Petersburg, FL 33702
    Telephone (813) 579-1111; Fax (813) 578-2178

AbraTrak is a stand-alone software program. It works in conjunction with AbraScan, both part of a series of human resource management programs by this company, which includes a human resource management system and an integrated payroll system.

▶ *AM/2000:* Spectrum Human Resource Systems Corporation, 1625 Broadway, Suite 2700, Denver, CO 80202
    Telephone (303) 534-8813; Fax (303) 595-9970

AM/2000 helps track applicants and requisitions with more than 800 fields of information. The PC-based, scanner-compatible system permits employers to identify candidates by key criteria, as well as to produce job postings, letters, and management reports. AM/2000 is designed to interact with other human resource programs available from this company.

▶ *ATS-Pro:* Human Resource MicroSystems, 160 Sansome Street, Suite 1450, San Francisco, CA 94104
  Telephone (800) 972-8470 or (415) 362-8400; Fax (415) 362-8595

ATS-Pro is an applicant tracking system that is available as a standalone product or as a module top HRIS-Pro, which is a comprehensive human resource system. It permits job and applicant matching based on user-defined criteria. The system monitors applicant flow and generates letters and interview schedules.

▶ *Exxis:* Exxis Corporation, P.O. Box 10718, Phoenix, AZ 85064
  Telephone (800) 243-9947; Fax (602) 274-0428

Exxis Corporation markets this low-cost applicant tracking system for use on the PC. It offers most of the tools available on more powerful systems. The company's ExxScan scanning system permits the user to enter selected personnel data directly from a resume into the human resource database. The program offers fully integrated modular systems for applicant tracking, employee tracking, job requisition management, and most government-required reports.

▶ *Genesys Human Resource System:* Genesys Software Systems, 5 Branch Street, Methuen, MA 01844
  Telephone (508) 685-5400; Fax (508) 683-7665

The Genesys Human Resource System is a comprehensive online information system that makes applicant tracking and staffing simple. Employers use the Genesys data entry screens to add contract information, equal employment opportunity demographics, job skills, work history, and comments made by the interviewer, and to generate offer or rejection letters. When an applicant is hired, the applicant's status is changed to employee and all the information becomes part of the employee database.

▶ *Human Resource Information Center:* Computing Management, Inc., 2346 South Lynhurst Drive, Suite C-101, Indianapolis, IN 46241
  Telephone (317) 247-4485; Fax (317) 247-0153

Part of this package system involves applicant tracking. Operating similar to other programs, Human Resource Information Center generates letters, forms, and reports, and maintains data necessary to conform to government affirmative action requirements.

▶ *PeopleSoft:* PeopleSoft, Inc., 1331 North California Boulevard, Walnut Creek, CA 94596
     Telephone (510) 946-9460; Fax (510) 946-9461

Representatives of the PeopleSoft Human Resource Management System (PS/HRMS) say their program offers a comprehensive and timely applicant tracking capability. By streamlining and automating the recruiting process, the program enables the user to process large volumes of applications and resumes.

PeopleSoft has the ability to perform online searches of the database for applicants with specific qualifications in such areas as education, skills, test scores, and licensing.

Additionally, this system can monitor applicant hiring expenses.

PeopleSoft says its program makes the interview process easier because the system can automatically set up an interview schedule for the applicant. The system will generate acknowledgment and regret letters, and it can post new job openings.

▶ *PowerMatch:* PowerMatch, 625 Ellis Street, Suite 303, Mountain View, CA 94043
     Telephone (415) 962-1425; Fax (415) 965-2686

One of the newest applicant tracking systems on the market, PowerMatch is a comprehensive employment management software program. PowerMatch offers the flexibility of operating on either IBM-PCs and compatibles or on Apple's Macintosh.

PowerMatch searches for any word in a full-text search, rather than using precoded search words. This system offers optical character recognition (OCR) and fax OCR capabilities. PowerMatch has most of the other features offered by some of the more popular systems, but "at considerably less cost," PowerMatch officials say.

Although PowerMatch is capable of running on an IBM-PC or compatible 286 or a comparable Apple Macintosh, company officials recommend a compatible 386 or 486 or a comparable Mac.

▶ *Restrac Employment Management System:* MicroTrac Systems, Inc., 1 Dedham Place, Dedham, MA 02026
     Telephone (617) 320-5600; Fax (617) 320-5630

The principal components of Restrac, an industry leader, include a resume scanning and retrieval system and a structured employment management database for tracking applicants through the hiring process. A series of add-on module programs are available to enhance the system's functions. This program is designed to operate within the Microsoft Windows software programming on any IBM-PC or compatible computer. This system generates not only applicant letters, but envelopes and mailing labels as well.

▶ *Resumate:* Resumate, Inc., P.O. Box 7438, Ann Arbor, MI 48107
   Telephone (800) 530-9310; Fax (313) 429-4228

Resumate's applicant tracking system offers low-cost programming (less than $2,200) that can run on virtually any IBM-PC or compatible computer system. Company officials point out that its simplicity is another cost savings in that it eliminates another major expense: employee training.

Resumate officials say customizing this program is easily accomplished in minutes.

▶ *Resumix:* Resumix, Inc., 2953 Bunker Hill Lane, Santa Clara, CA 95054
   Telephone (408) 562-4444; Fax (408) 727-9893

Resumix is one of the leaders in the automated tracking industry. Regardless of format, each resume is processed. The system extracts and analyzes information to provide an applicant summary for the interviewer or hiring manager. Resumix can store job requirements that are matched automatically against any resume currently in the database or any new resumes that are scanned into the system.

▶ *SmartSearch2:* Advanced Personnel Systems, 4167 Avenida De La Plata, Suite 126, Oceanside, CA 92056
   Telephone (619) 757-1055; Fax (619) 757-1054

SmartSearch2 is a "total recall with perfect precision" system. Another industry leader, SmartSearch2 has a feature allowing the computer to "learn" every word scanned into the system. It is the only product that tailors its search dictionary to each client's unique recruiting needs. The automatic letter-generating feature not only writes the acknowledgment or regret letter, but imprints signatures.

THE WAVE OF THE FUTURE

Applicant tracking systems are where the big action is in the electronic recruitment revolution.

A Texas systems manager puts it into perspective when he says human resource personnel are not functioning in a radically different way from manual systems, but they are "functioning more quickly and efficiently. It's like trading in a horse for a car."

4

Armchair Job Hunting

Online Ads That Jump Out of Corporate America and onto Your Computer Screen

In the last two chapters, we examined databases that contain resumes—people.

In this chapter, we look at the jobs side of the coin as we consider electronic resources for actual advertised job openings—the classified help-wanted ads you find on your computer screen.

Attention, job applicants! Get ready for the Digital Decade. Welcome to another face of computer-driven job search in the 1990s—the hunt for employers who can hire you.

Electronic prowling, one of the bright spots in the new rules of searching for jobs, will fatten your bank balance and enrich your life. It's a bright spot because, if you get lucky, electronics actually can lighten your load in a hard-hitting job search campaign.

In these times of 12-hour-a-day marathon job hunts, any productive activity that allows you to put your feet up for a little while is worth doing.

It used to be enough to search for job openings through the daily newspaper. People who were industrious scouted the trade journals as well. Some job seekers used job services, learning quickly that the employment agencies to register with were those operating on an employer-paid-fee basis.

Several decades ago, job applicants learned how to network—that is, how to make a spiderweb of contacts and skulk through the "hidden" job market, the one where employers kept mum about their hiring needs until job openings were pried out of them.

Now, in an increasingly complex world and a chaotic job market, electronics comes to the rescue in the drive to uncover job leads.

No matter how splendiferous your resume or superb your interviewing skills, your challenge is to search out and pinpoint where the jobs are.

In sales work, this task is like developing a prospect list. In fund raising, it's creating a contributor base. In politics, it's identifying the committed voters. In any situation, it's a VID—Very Important Detail—and a priority assignment.

With today's electronic aids, this VID usually starts with a personal computer, a modem, and communications software. A modem is the "machine," and the software is the "driver" that lets you hook up with another computer.

Assuming you have a computer, you can purchase an inexpensive modem. Most modems in use today are 2400, 9600, or 14,400 BPS (bits per second). The higher the BPS rate, the faster the telecommunications and the more expensive the modem. Modems that telecommunicate at 2400 BPS are advertised at $50 to $100; you can buy a 9600 or 14,400 BPS modem for a little more than $200.

If you already have a modem, chances are you have a communications software program. All you need to do is call your online service of choice, sign up and get issued a password, and then follow the service's instructions.

If you've been shopping to buy a computer and modem, you've probably seen how computer hardware prices are plunging as more and more Americans are plugging into home computing.

What if you don't have a computer and a modem, don't like them, don't want them, and never want to hear another word about them? That's okay. You need not tune your brain to the world of computers. You can hire someone to search for you.

If that's your plan, buy another copy of this book and give it to the job search electronic researcher you hire. (Chapter 5 will help you find one.) The researcher can then clue in on the degree of sophistication you expect in the job search product you're buying.

Your own copy of the book will remind you of the quality of information you expect the researcher to deliver and the questions you should be asking: "Did you use this database? . . . Did you use that online service? . . . Where did the data come from?" And so on. You need not make yourself into a computer whiz, but you ought to know what you're buying.

Let's assume this job search is a do-it-yourself project. One common way to turn your computer into a job search tool is by using an online information service.

ONLINE INFORMATION SERVICES

We've used the term "online" frequently in earlier chapters. It merely means a computer is hooked by telephone to giant silos of data. Your own computer, with incredible speed and accuracy, can descend into the silo you've selected and home in on exactly the kernel of knowledge you've asked for. Within seconds, it will be readable on your computer screen.

When you are online, your computer is linked to another computer and the machines are having a chat.

Classified help-wanted ads and other employment information often are transmitted over "online information services," which resemble cable television's programming services of news, comedy, music, talk, movies, and so forth. Unlike cable, which requires a monthly fee, most online services are pay-as-you-go after the initial sign-up fee.

You choose from a whole menu of categories when you use online information services. Employment is only one category. But for you, the job hunter, it's by far the most important! Here's why:

▶ Through online information services, you receive data about job openings offered by electronic job ad companies and nonprofit organizations.

▶ Through online information services, you reach various employment-related databases and informal employment bulletin boards provided by the online information services to their subscribers.

▶ As an alternative to using online information services, you can gain direct access to stand-alone job services.

If you live in a metropolitan area, you may be able to call online services free or at very low cost because many of them have either local telephone numbers or toll-free 800 numbers.

Whatever the telephone charges to access an online job service, you will need to find the correct telephone number and, in some cases, obtain a password.

Membership in online information services generally isn't free. You can't just call up and plug in. But you can join for a small monthly subscription fee. The amount of the fee varies from service to service and changes from time to time.

Information coverage and prices differ enough to make it worth your time to comparison shop.

The big online services probably offer a larger platter of information than you'll use, and the sheer volume can be confusing. The small services usually are easier to use and less expensive, but may not have everything you need.

In addition to a nominal monthly subscription fee (usually billed automatically to your credit card), many online information services charge for each minute you spend "connected" online in certain categories. (Some categories are billed by the "connected" minute; others are free no matter how long you are connected.)

In addition to the monthly fee and possible connection charges, you have to pay telecommunications charges. There will be no telephone line charges to local access numbers or to 800 numbers (if you pay a flat telephone rate).

If you can't call on a local or an 800 telephone access number, you'll have to pay per-minute toll or long-distance telecommunications charges to the nearest access number. Long-distance telecommunications charges are only 25 cents or less per minute during day hours, and 13 cents or less during night hours.

You may or may not have to pay a modest fee for an online service's start-up kit. As we pointed out earlier, often the start-up kit is included as a bonus item in the purchase of telecommunications hardware such as a modem. Some online services charge for the start-up kit but throw in the first month's subscription fee as part of the package.

Costs can vary widely. Call any service in which you are interested, and obtain a description of the information covered, literature, costs, and, if available, a demonstration of the software.

To recap: The costs of using an online information service to hunt for job openings fall into four possible areas:

1. A monthly subscription fee. (Call the service to determine cost; it may be free.)
2. A connection charge for each minute you are online to specific categories. (Remember, many categories of data are free.)
3. A telecommunications charge. (Usually the cost is only 25 cents or less per minute; it may be free.)

4. A software start-up kit fee. (Usually the kit is inexpensive; often, it's free.)

For a complete listing of online information services, ask at your library for the 1,300-page *Gale Directory of Databases, Volume 1.* This excellent library reference book offers unparalleled scope and depth; there simply isn't a comparable resource available.

Here are some of the larger online information services we've found to have useful employment categories.

▶ *CompuServe:* CompuServe Incorporated, 5000 Arlington Centre Boulevard, P.O. Box 20212, Columbus, OH 43220
Telephone (800) 848-8199; Fax (614) 457-0348

CompuServe provides a wide range of moderately priced databases including some that are likely to be useful in a job search.

Like other online services, CompuServe provides several news databases, such as Reuters, Associated Press, Business Wire, and *The Washington Post.* Full-text newspaper coverage is limited compared to other services. For company data, CompuServe's available databases include Value Line financial statements, Standard & Poor's company information, and Investext investment analyst research reports. A host of special interest forums offer ongoing opportunities to network a particular subject; you might, for instance, find out about an engineering position by networking with other engineers.

Members of CompuServe Information Service can search for jobs in CompuServe's classifieds area. The modest monthly fee gives you unlimited connect-time access to 36 basic services, one of which is classifieds. The ads are provided by E-Span, a major job ad service described below.

The Knowledge Index is a nighttime and weekend option offered at a reduced rate compared to the charge during daytime business hours. Although accessed through CompuServe, it is not included in the monthly fee but is billed by the hour. It contains abstracts of more than 50,000 journals, many of which include the full text of the articles, and in excess of 100 databases. The Knowledge Index has become a prime source of information for professionals who conduct their own research. One of the databases is Standard & Poor's Corporate Register.

▶ *Dialog:* Dialog Information Services, 3460 Hillview Avenue, Palo Alto, CA 94304
Telephone (800) 334-2564; Fax (415) 858-7069

This online information service offers more than 400 databases with broad subject coverage, such as agriculture, biology, biotechnology, business and corporate news, chemistry, computers, drugs, economics, energy/environment, engineering, government, humanities, law, medicine, patents and trademarks, science and technology, social sciences, and general reference.

For literature searches, Dialog has abstracts of more than 50,000 journals with at least 2,500 journals, newsletters, and magazines in full text online, as well as 150 newspapers. A few examples: *Los Angeles Times, Boston Globe, USA Today,* and *Business Wire* databases contain full-text coverage.

Other categories, such as the National Newspaper Index, the Legal Resource Index, and the Computer Database, contain abstract information. Executive biographies are available from Marquis Who's Who.

Query the company for details of useful data.

▶ *GEnie:* General Electric Network for Information Exchange, 401 North Washington Street, Rockville, MD 20850
Telephone (800) 638-9636

Despite the word "network" in the company name, this is an online information service. It carries a number of useful features that will interest job seekers and career managers.

E-Span, the job ad online service discussed later in this chapter, can be accessed on GEnie.

GEnie carries other services described elsewhere in this book, including the Business Resource Directory (Chapter 5), and Dr. Job and the Home Office/Small Business RoundTable (both in Chapter 7).

▶ *Prodigy:* Prodigy Services Company, 445 Hamilton Avenue, White Plains, NY 10601
Telephone (800) PRODIGY

This moderately priced service provides access to online classifieds and a careers bulletin board.

The careers bulletin board is not a job listing but a way to electronically do "informational interviewing": you ask people in the job field you're investigating to comment and offer referrals. Members can leave messages about occupations they're considering entering and ask that other members already in that occupation get back to them.

ONLINE JOB AD COMPANIES

As we mentioned earlier, individual online job ad services are carried on the general online information services. These online job ad services are also called "job bulletin boards."

The job bulletin boards are presented by:

1. Companies specializing in electronic job ads.
2. Government agencies.
3. Professional societies and trade associations.
4. Industry publications.
5. Job services firms (recruiting agencies).
6. Ad hoc organizations operating as a public service.

Most services displaying electronic help-wanted ads deal with a wide assortment of occupations, or at least a wide assortment in a given career field. But some online job listings are narrowly restricted to certain occupations. For the restricted listings, you will need to be a member of a professional society or trade organization before you can use its job bulletin board.

An example of occupation-specific services is OT Source, an online service for occupational therapists, operated by the American Occupational Therapy Association (1383 Piccard Drive, Rockville, MD 20850; (800) 377-8555) or (301) 948-9626).

OT Source offers many topics of interest to occupational therapists, from new technology to regulatory actions. The one we're interested in is the Job Bank, which lists hundreds of occupational therapy related job openings across the nation. American Occupational Therapy Association members who use the online service pay a modest yearly charge; nonmembers also can subscribe but it costs them more.

Another example is the occupation-specific job bulletin board operated by the Society for Technical Communication (901 North Stuart Street, Suite 904, Arlington, VA 22203; (703) 522-4114).

The bulletin board usually holds some 75 openings for jobs ranging from technical writers to managers. Unless the Society for Technical Communication hears that a position is filled, the listing stays online for two months. Some local chapters maintain bulletin boards of technical jobs in their areas.

Scores of online services are in operation and more are on the way. What follows is a group of services illustrating those that specialize in job ads, also called help-wanted ads, recruitment ads, job

Finding and Choosing Online Job Ad Services

Library reference directories aren't the only places where you can chase after job bulletin boards. Try these approaches:

▶ Call any professional society to which you belong. If the society doesn't have an online job ad service, perhaps the time is ripe to start one.

▶ Ask at your college's career center and alumni office.

▶ Page through professional and trade publications, as well as computer magazines such as Computer Shopper, a monthly sold nationwide on newsstands; it contains references to various bulletin boards.

Some local free publications, such as San Diego's ComputerEdge, list bulletin boards, most of which have nothing to do with jobs but you never know when one will turn up.

Another free publication, Computer Currents, lists bulletin boards and is available in a number of large cities. Computer stores usually have copies in racks and you can just pick them up.

One of the problems with a bulletin board system (BBS) run by volunteers is the upkeep. It may become too much of a chore and the BBS goes dead or at least gets very tired.

You want a job BBS that's continually updated and used by enthusiastic, dedicated people. Look for current dates on the screen and notice how many new postings were made since the last time you logged in. A telephone busy signal when you try to get into the job bulletin board isn't a benchmark: It may mean the system is popular because it's good, or it may indicate the bulletin board has a system malfunction.

If you'd like more information on how online information services work, as well as other wonders of the electronic universe, read *Get On-Line! The Communications Software Companion* by Lamont Wood (John Wiley & Sons, 1993). This book is for readers who aren't interested in a glob of technical trivia but want answers in a hurry.

When accessing an online service, unless otherwise instructed, set your modem software to "8 data bits," "No parity," and "1 stop bit." Then dial your number.

listings, or job postings. (Purists find differences in these terms, but most people use them interchangeably.)

▶ *Access . . . FCO On-Line:* Federal Research Service, Inc., 243 Church Street N.W., Vienna, VA 22180
    Telephone (703) 281-0200; Fax (703) 281-7639

Access is an online service of Federal Research Service, Inc., publishers of a print publication of federal career employment announcements (job openings). The listing contains about 4,000 jobs in Uncle Sam's government. The service is updated every weekday with new job listings.
    Available 24 hours a day, this service offers one of the most efficient ways to get current information on federal job openings. You pay an initial set-up fee plus an hourly connect charge. Your account remains active for one year from the date of your last order. Technical staff is available to answer questions about using this service.
    You can search by many criteria, such as job level, agency, location, or occupational specialty.
    Users in most locations outside the Washington, DC, area can enter the system locally, avoiding long-distance charges.

▶ *America Online:* America Online, Inc., 8619 Westwood Center Drive, Vienna, VA 22182
    Telephone (800) 827-6364; Fax (703) 883-1509

America Online is a leading independent provider of online services to consumers in the United States. It offers subscribers a wide variety of services, including e-mail, conferencing, computing support, and online classes to help upgrade users' online abilities.
    This service, founded in 1985, carries several newspaper online services, as well as an electronic Career Center. Both are described more fully in Chapter 7.

▶ *Career Doctors Bulletin Board Service:* Executive Directions, 2 Penn Plaza, Suite 1185, New York, NY 10121
    Telephone (212) 594-5775; Fax (212) 594-4183; Modem (up to 2400 BPS) (212) 279-4855; Modem (up to 9600 BPS) (212) 279-4875

Experienced computer and information systems specialists who use Career Doctors BBS are getting straight through to a technical recruiting firm, which may be one of your target resources.
    The service is free to job seekers but they must pay telephone charges.

With this service, you can search for job listings by state or by a variety of other criteria. You can also send your resume by computer hookup to apply for positions. No resume? No problem. You can apply for a particular position by filling out a temporary mini-resume and sending it online until you get a full-blown version ready.

Career Doctors BBS operates 24 hours a day, 7 days a week. Among its other features are job hunting tips and technical conferences. Computer pros, modem on in.

▶ *Career Link Worldwide:* P.O. Box 11720, Phoenix, AZ 85061
Telephone (800) 453-3350; Fax (602) 841-5981;
Modem (602) 973-2002

Since 1984, Career Link Worldwide has maintained a global online computer job database. It contains 2,500 job openings. Of that number, about 2,100 are jobs in the United States and 400 are jobs overseas. The company says 600 new job listings are added each week.

Each job listing shows the job title and job description, and the hiring company's address and fax number.

At no cost (except long-distance telephone charges), job seekers can try Career Link Worldwide before buying. A sample database of 200 jobs is offered; however, all of the sample jobs are a little long in the tooth—perhaps six months old. Look at the free sample as a kind of dress rehearsal in which you practice using an online service—accessing and downloading (printing out the database on your computer). For computer neophytes, this is a good offer.

After evaluating the free sample, if you decide you want to subscribe to the actual database of 2,500 current job listings, it will cost you from 25 cents to 50 cents per minute, depending on how fast your modem runs, to download as much as you want. The most you could pay to download the entire existing database is about $30.

This database is reported to be quite current.

▶ *Career Network:* 640 North LaSalle Street, Suite 560, Chicago, IL 60610
Telephone (800) 229-6499; Fax (312) 642-0616

Turning now to on-campus electronic job listing and advertising, the national Career Network turns college career centers into a gold mine of employment information for students and graduates at a dozen colleges in America. Among them are Indiana University, Harvard University, the University of Houston, and Brigham Young University. The company plans to quickly expand to 100 more institutions of higher education.

This campus online service operates through Prodigy, which has more than 1.5 million subscribers who access it with user-friendly software on their personal modem-equipped computers.

Sponsored by such blue chips as Aetna, Alcoa, Burlington Industries, Continental Insurance, Deloitte & Touche, Eli Lilly, General Electric, IBM, Monsanto Chemical, Motorola, Nissan, Procter & Gamble, and Sears, Career Network offers online job postings that students can access from their dorm or home, as well as from the campus career center.

Experienced alumni can access Career Network from their offices or homes anywhere in the country, simply by entering the service through a local telephone number—and, of course, their assigned password.

By using a nationwide online computer network (Prodigy), Career Network provides e-mail communications between employers and the schools' placement offices.

Students can access current industry information through online bulletin boards, or on-campus online job postings from their school's career center, their dorms, or their homes. Experienced alumni looking for work or for a better career position can access the online information from their offices or homes anywhere in the nation.

Job openings, should, theoretically, be current on the Career Network because the technology allows employers to easily update

Abbreviations Often Used in Online Job Ads

AA	Affirmative action
BA	Bachelor of arts degree
BS	Bachelor of science degree
BSBA	Bachelor of science in business administration
CNE	Certified network engineer
CPA	Certified public accountant
DOD	Department of Defense
DOE	Department of Energy
EOE	Equal opportunity employer
MBA	Master of business administration degree
MS	Master of science degree
M/F/D/V	Male/female/disabled/veteran

Courtesy of E-Span JobSearch

the information at a moment's notice. (By contrast, job openings posted on a campus bulletin board may be dated and many of the jobs may be already filled.)

▶ *Classifacts:* North American Classifacts, 50 South Steel Street, Suite 222, Denver, CO 80209
    Telephone (303) 322-0711; Fax (303) 321-7089

This service is a national database of newspaper classified ads, supplied quickly and directly by the newspapers themselves.

Classifacts allows job seekers to pick up the telephone and instantly obtain classified ads from almost any major U.S. newspaper market. Approximately 60 newspapers are reported to have signed to supply their ads to Classifacts. Among the classified offerings in this giant marketplace, consumers will find everything from automobiles to real estate. Job seekers will select help-wanted ads related to specific occupations or geographic areas.

The process begins when job seekers call the Classifacts number to buy four-week subscriptions to job ads in their occupational area of interest. They can select ads placed anywhere in the country.

Speedy computers search all the ads from all the newspapers and report those of interest to the job seekers. A timely printout of the ads is delivered by surface mail, overnight mail, fax, or modem, and follow-up reports are delivered for three additional weeks. You could say, for instance, "I want to see everything for dental hygienists in Los Angeles, or in the New England states."

Classifacts may prove to be among the most valuable tools for long-distance job hunts, because you don't have to subscribe to a dozen newspapers. The newspapers are participating in electronic pooling of their classified ads, so you have a reasonable chance to contact employers before the ads become stale and the job openings they describe are filled.

▶ *Computerworld Careers On-Line:* P.O. Box 880, Framingham, MA 01701
    Telephone (508) 879-0700; Fax (508) 875-8931;
Modem (508) 879-4700

Some online services are targeted to specific occupational groups. A prime example is Computerworld Careers On-Line, a service of the weekly publication, *Computerworld*. It speaks to information systems professionals.

To extend life to *Computerworld*'s print recruitment advertising, the publication throws in four weeks of online job posting with every print ad. As a second feature, job seekers can view *Computerworld*'s recruitment ads and post their resumes on the service. A template is offered, which prompts job seekers to complete a basic experience-and-skills history. Employers are encouraged to download and review resumes of job seekers who have the profile the employer is seeking.

Neither the employer nor the job seeker pays for the electronic services.

▶ *Drei Tauben Ltd.:* 137 Highland Avenue, Jersey City, NJ 07306
   Telephone (908) 876-4835; Fax (908) 876-4836;
Modem (908) 613-0500

The company name means "three pigeons" in German. The inspiration came from the fact that some of the earliest information services used pigeons as messengers, and sometimes sent two, or even three, for reliability. Add to that the fact that the firm was founded by a trio of graduates of Stevens Institute of Technology, and three pigeons it is.

The firm's computerized job service is called "Allée," which is French for "pathway." The cosmopolitan titles hint at the innovative culture of this young East Coast firm, which offers job ads free to anyone in the nation who has a computer and modem.

Most of the ads are aimed at people who can handle technology—experienced engineering, science, technical, and management professionals.

The jobs listed, thus far, are concentrated in computer science, pharmaceuticals, environmental science, and construction.

Drei Tauben advertisers get two computer screens of information to describe each job, and another screen to describe themselves as employers and the community where they're located. The ads remain on the system for 28 days.

Spreading the word to high demand technology specialists is accomplished by working through college alumni associations and advertising in technical publications. The company says the service has grown into a nationwide operation involving 130 of the top engineering colleges and universities, organized as the University Employment Consortium.

To peruse the job listings, merely call the modem number above at any time of day or night, seven days a week. The cost to the job seeker is only the telephone charge to make the connection.

▸ *E-Span:* 8440 Woodfield Crossing, Suite 170, Indianapolis, IN 46240
Telephone (800) 682-2901 or (317) 469-4535; Fax (317) 469-4508

Together, E-Span JobSearch and E-Span Online Access are said to form the nation's largest provider of employment advertising delivered to personal home computers over national PC online services.

According to E-Span, if you sign up, you'll be joining 4 million subscribers who have the opportunity to peruse the listed job openings. These subscribers are reportedly college-educated, computer-literate, professional, managerial, and technically proficient.

For this cream of the crop, the hopeful winds of career advancement are said to be blowing—now, or when the right job comes along.

By tapping into E-Span through one of the online job ad companies' carriers, such as CompuServe or Prodigy, you can browse job opportunities advertised by hundreds of Fortune 1000 companies. You select from more than two dozen categories and then narrow your search by geographic location.

Job listings are available for specific regions of the United States, as well as for Canada and countries throughout the world. The E-Span databases are updated weekly, and advertisements generally run for two weeks.

When you spot a job you think has your name on it, you contact the employer directly, sending your resume via the U.S. Postal Service, e-mail, or fax. Or, if the advertisement so directs, you contact the employer by telephone. (The numbers are listed above.)

E-Span JobSearch advertisers have the option of providing a corporate profile along with their job listings. The advertisers contract directly with E-Span to display job openings.

E-Span Online Access is an extension of newspaper help-wanted ads. An advertiser places a print help-wanted ad with a newspaper; the newspaper not only prints the ad but, as a value-added service, contracts with E-Span to carry the ad electronically. Advertisers like the combination package because it more widely circulates their recruitment message.

Job seekers should look through both E-Span services. (E-Span also operates a resume service, the Candidate Database, but its chief effort is in job openings.)

▸ *Federal Job Opportunities Board:* Office of Personnel Management, Staffing Service Center, 4685 Log Cabin Drive, Macon, GA 31298
FJOB Modem (912) 757-3100

"All of Uncle Sam's jobs in one place"—that's a quick description of this government bulletin board service. It includes both current job openings and expected future job openings, labeled as "opportunities."

Once you dial into the system with your PC/modem/communications software, you're told what to do next. The Federal Job Opportunities Board operates like most other online information services. It runs on what is termed a "menu driven" format, which merely means it's step-by-step; if you can read, you can do it.

You will be asked to provide some basic personal information to qualify as a "registered user."

The database is updated every night, which makes it one of the freshest information sources around. Using a job series number or job title, you can search the entire database of every federal job opening and potential job opening for specific positions. You have the option of specifying the government grade level and the state in which the job is located.

The job series number is the number assigned by the federal government to each occupation. When you are in the system, you can activate the help feature and see all the occupations and their corresponding numbers. It's not difficult to use.

If you are not familiar with the job series numbering system, you can search by job title. For instance, if you want to look in the law enforcement area, you might key in the word *law* or *officer*.

For computer specialist, computer programmer, or computer analyst, you might key in the word *compute*. Jobs under all these occupational categories will flash on your screen.

The Federal Job Opportunities Board doesn't stop with job listings. It also issues bulletins that explain the role of the Office of Personnel Management in helping you find your way through the maze of federal employment. The service also details federal salary tables.

An alternative to searching nationwide for federal jobs is to confine your hunt to a particular state. You may prefer to access the Regional Office of Personnel Management Bulletin Boards. You won't get as much information, but you'll spend less money on telephone bills—and some calls won't even be long-distance. The offices usually are closed on weekends.

Here is a list of Regional Office of Personnel Management Bulletin Boards and their telephone numbers:

Atlanta Bulletin Board/Voice	(404) 331-3459
Atlanta Bulletin Board/Modem	(404) 730-2370
Dallas Bulletin Board/Voice	(214) 767-8245

Dallas Bulletin Board/Modem (1200/2400 BPS)	(214) 767-0565
Dallas Bulletin Board/Modem (9600 BPS)	(214) 767-5471
Detroit Bulletin Board/Voice	(313) 226-6950
Detroit Bulletin Board/Modem (2400 BPS)	(313) 226-4423
Philadelphia Bulletin Board/Modem (1200/2400 BPS)	(215) 580-2216
Philadelphia Bulletin Board/Modem	(201) 645-3887

Federal job information is also available at public employment service offices through the Federal Employment Data Services System. You do not operate this system but request a public employment service employee to assist you.

A related and very impressive system you do operate yourself is the Federal Job Information Touchscreen Computer System. It's found at college career centers and job fairs, as well as at public employment service offices.

You just walk right up and touch color blocks on the computer's screen to select the information you want. The system answers back with key points highlighted by the computer's synthetic voice component. If you want the information immediately printed out, all you have to do is finger another block on the screen.

You can search for jobs by state or nationwide, and enter your name and address on the touchscreen to request application forms and materials.

The system gives you a variety of information on federal employment, including announcements about current federal career opportunities, how the hiring process works, and federal jobs for which you may qualify. No moss grows on the touchscreen system—like the Federal Job Opportunities Board and the Federal Employment Data Services System, it's changed daily.

▶ *Job Ads USA:* Militran, Inc., 1255 Drummers Lane, Suite 306, Wayne, PA 19087
Telephone (215) 687-3900; Fax (215) 296-7332

Job Ads USA collects help-wanted ads across the nation and displays them over the Human Resource Information Network, the computer electronics carrier specific to human resource departments.

Human resource professionals use the job ads as a tool for placing employees who are out the door in downsizing cuts or the spouses of employees who are relocating within a company.

The database, a roundup of job openings during the most recent six weeks, is collected from more than 100 newspaper classified help-wanted sections. Other listings of civil service job openings come from the federal government's Office of Personnel Management.

Each of the newspaper ads shows the publication name and date, as well as an abstract of the original classified ad. The online database can be searched by publication date, job title, job classification, and military occupational codes.

▶ *Jobtrac:* 6856 Arboreal Drive, Dallas, TX 75231
No voice telephone; Modem (214) 349-0527

This online job ad service is operated by volunteers out of the goodness of their hearts and is free to users. A small contribution is welcome and will be used to update the equipment. The jobs listed range across the board and, although more concentrated in the Greater Dallas–Fort Worth area, can be located anywhere in the nation.

There's quite a story behind this job bulletin board. When Braniff Airlines went into a financial tailspin in 1985, Kerry Goodwin took action. Goodwin, who was president of the Dallas Alliance of Business, asked H. Ross Perot if several programmers at his Electronic Data Systems company could assist in creating software for a bulletin board system to help 3,000 of the airline's employees find new jobs. It worked! That service, Jobtrac, continues to this day, operated by a half-dozen selfless volunteers, still quarterbacked by Kerry Goodwin.

It banners jobs in a spectrum of occupational fields: accounting, administrative, education, engineering, medical, nonprofit, professional, sales, secretarial, and technical careers.

There's more. Jobtrac gives you federal employment opportunities in the state of Texas, including jobs with the SuperCollider, and identifies about two dozen nationwide job bulletin boards.

Goodwin says, "We accept jobs from anywhere that people want to list." Job seekers can contact employers directly (best way) or modem back their resumes.

Jobtrac offers information on job search topics ranging from writing resumes to a program that helps you fill out the federal government's SF-171 job application form. This is a real public service and you should remember to say "Thank you."

▶ *Jobtrak:* 1990 Westwood Boulevard, Suite 260, Los Angeles, CA 90025
Telephone (310) 474-3377; Fax (310) 475-7912

Another popular college-oriented online recruitment service operates with a different twist. Jobtrak is really a variation of the online computer service: each day, it transmits job listings by modem to college career centers.

At the colleges, the job listings are given maximum exposure to students and alumni. The information is printed and posted on bulletin boards, displayed on computer terminals, heard on telephone-based job lines, and sometimes printed in job bulletins.

Jobtrak, headquartered in Los Angeles, sends job listings from thousands of major corporations and small businesses to more than 200 colleges nationwide. With one telephone call, employers are able to list their full-time, part-time, professional, and nonprofessional positions at their choice of colleges. The service says that, since 1989, more than 60,000 companies have used Jobtrak to advertise job opportunities.

Among its big-name customers are: Allstate Insurance, American Express, AT&T, Bank of America, Hughes Aircraft, IBM, Kinney Shoes, Ramada Hotels, Sears, and Xerox.

Jobtrak is provided free to colleges on its network. Employers pay a small fee to list positions.

How effective is Jobtrack? The service says 15 of its own employees were hired through listings placed at colleges. Corporate college recruiters and college career center directors highly recommend it.

▶ *LA Online:* 332 Hermosa Avenue, Suite 7, Hermosa Beach, CA 90254

Telephone (310) 372-9364; Modem (310) 372-4050

LA Online is an online database serving Los Angeles. Along with shopping, news, and regular features, it includes two sections useful to job seekers.

The first gives users access to the classified help-wanted ads from Los Angeles' largest community publications.

You simply type "Go News," select the publication of your choice, and pull up the classified listing in each newspaper.

On-line Career Fair is the second selection job seekers can choose. These are job listings not taken from newspapers but directly posted to the LA Online. The size of On-line Career Fair goes up and down with the job climate. At times, only a dozen or so jobs are posted; at other times, thousands of jobs are noted.

Access to LA Online is free.

▶ *Networking Careers On-Line:* Network World Bulletin Board System, 161 Worcester Road, Framingham, MA 01701

Telephone (800) 622-1108; Fax (508) 879-3167; Modem (up to 2400 BPS) (508) 620-1160; Modem (up to 9600 BPS) (508) 620-1178

Computer and computer networking specialists make between 4,000 and 6,000 calls monthly to this service, which mirrors the job ads in *Network World* magazine. Except for telephone charges, the online job ad service is free to job seekers.

The job bulletin board carries a full month's worth of ads from the magazine, plus information about companies' corporate backgrounds. By using the bulletin board, you can get a head start on magazine readers because the jobs are posted electronically on Friday and printed the following Monday.

Networking Careers On-Line accepts resumes electronically and faxes them to employers. Other service features include a career forum where participants share information and advice about career opportunities and employment-related subjects.

▶ ***On-Line Career Fair:*** Response Technologies Corporation, Two Campton Commons, Campton, NH 03223
Telephone (603) 726-4800; Fax (603) 726-3909; Modem (603) 726-3344

On-Line Career Fair is the product of Response Technologies Corporation. The nationwide service is targeted to job seekers in the fields of computers, engineering, sales/marketing, and finance. Job seekers learn about the online service through Response Technologies Corporation ads in various newspapers, trade journals, and professional society publications.

Employers seeking to recruit personnel in the target fields often place their own print job ads with an invitation to respond through the On-Line Career Fair service.

The service is free to job seekers. After dialing into the modem, you merely press "enter" twice and type the password "new job." This enables you to see all the job listings in the entire service.

You can submit a resume directly to the companies of your choice by computer-modem, by fax, or by mail.

Employers who run their own print recruitment ads routing readers through On-Line Career Fair include in print a private password that zooms in on the advertiser's electronic job listings.

Interleaf, a software company, for instance, uses the password "hire me." Job seekers responding to print ads placed by Interleaf are invited to dial On-Line Career Fair, enter the password, and get details on openings in sales, foreign language software development, consulting, project management, and technical publications.

The On-Line Career Fair details will be far more extensive than those found in print recruitment advertising.

After a Two-Year Job Hunt:
"If Only I Had Known about Online Job Search Sooner"

Barry Smiraglia worked for the Tandy Corporation (Radio Shack) for nearly 15 years, more than 11 as a store manager. He moved up in the Tandy organization to a new opening as a computer specialist in Nashua, New Hampshire. But, in a disappointing development, Smiraglia was laid off after a couple of years on the job. For Smiraglia, the worst wasn't over—he was out of work for two long years.

"I probably wouldn't have been out of work had I stayed a store manager," says Smiraglia. "But the opportunities computer work offers are wide-ranging, and I wanted to be a part of a career field that is moving forward."

A few years ago, the computer specialist had no idea just how much of an effect the computers he loved would ultimately have on his job search.

During most of those two years looking for employment, Smiraglia used traditional methods, unaware of the job search revolution computers are powering. He managed only part-time, seasonal work with his former employer. Finally, Smiraglia found a job as a software technical support specialist with business-form maker New England Business Service's (NEBS) newest accounting software program division, One Write Plus.

He found it through an electronic job ad service—On-Line Career Fair.

"I think I would have found employment much sooner had I known about jobs being available on [electronics] bulletin board systems," says Smiraglia. "By the time a job opening hits the newspaper, the competition is crushing."

But it was from a newspaper—The Nashua Telegraph—that Smiraglia actually found out about the NEBS job opening.

"I saw an ad NEBS had placed in the Sunday newspaper, which included an online BBS number to call for additional information," recalls Smiraglia. "I dialed in with my modem-equipped computer and the online service gave me a description of the company, as well as an opportunity to request additional information through the mail. It also allowed me the option of leaving my resume on the system."

Smiraglia chose to ask for additional information and found out about a job fair where he could meet and discuss possible employment with NEBS.

At the job fair, Smiraglia met Lorraine Falcone, a NEBS human resource specialist, who arranged an interview for him with a hiring manager. As a result, he was offered a job for which he is well-qualified and suited—not to mention one he truly enjoys.

"I'm excited about this opportunity," says Smiraglia, explaining that he offers telephone support and assistance to customers using the One Write Plus accounting software. "The computer is not only my life, it helped me find a great position. Online job searching with modem-equipped computer is definitely a powerful tool that will enhance anyone's job search."

In short, after the print ads generate interest, the electronic billboard takes over to more fully describe the available positions. The gain for Interleaf: Readers responding to its password will not have access to job listings on the remainder of the bulletin board. Interleaf will have their undivided attention—at far less cost than putting everything in print advertising.

▶ *Transition Bulletin Board:* For active duty personnel and their spouses, Military Installation Transition Offices;
For employers to register prior to listing jobs, (800) 727-3677

One of the biggest pools of job seekers today is the troops about to leave military life. A nationwide reduction in military personnel, combined with a tight civilian job market, has fueled the rapid growth of the Transition Assistance Program, a panel of outplacement programs now available on military bases around the globe.

For the Defense Outplacement Referral System (DORS) discussed in Chapter 2, the Transition Bulletin Board (TBB) is the other side of the coin.

DORS has people looking for jobs; TBB has jobs looking for people. Employers list job openings, and military personnel and their spouses read them on computer screens.

TBB helps military service members everywhere. For those stationed overseas, it's a godsend—almost like their hometown Sunday paper's classified help-wanted section coming straight to them. It gives service personnel in faraway lands, where they are cut off from the U.S. job market, a peek at what's available out there in civilianland.

Employers registered with Operation Transition are invited to insert free listings as well as their company's profile on this electronic bulletin board. Employers can enter the help-wanted ads by computer modem, or, lacking a modem, they can enter the ads by fax or mail. The job information is available the next business day to

Department of Defense personnel stationed at more than 350 military installations around the world. Military personnel respond directly to employers by sending resumes.

Like employers who peruse DORS, employers using TBB range from Fortune 500 companies to small businesses. They offer a variety of jobs from high-tech to blue-collar positions in the United States as well as overseas.

NEWSPAPER ONLINE INFORMATION SERVICES

Being newspaper people, we're popping our buttons to tell you that a number of North America's great papers are doing their share to bring you a world of information at prices that won't flatten your wallet.

Major newspaper companies are working together to find the best ways to deliver the news electronically. The Media Laboratory at Massachusetts Institute of Technology is conducting research for a consortium of newspapers, as well as for computer maker International Business Machines Corporation. This could lead to dramatic changes; already, newspapers are moving beyond the printed page through computer networks and telephone lines.

Newspapers were early pioneers in electronic services in the 1980s. The timing must not have been right because, in the main, they lost millions of dollars. Some call that era the newspaper industry's "Vietnam."

The deep hit in the pockets that newspapers took on early consumer electronic services left them shell-shocked. But now, according to reports from the Newspaper Association of America's Randy Bennett, interest appears to be growing in online services to supplement—not replace—the printed word.

The *Fort Worth Star-Telegram* is the industry standard-bearer for the longest, and generally profitable, operation of its online service, StarText.

Launched in 1982, StarText has undergone several reincarnations. Subscribers today can have an information picnic on StarText at a small charge per month for unlimited use.

Of the many StarText features, the number one and number two choices for job campaigners are the opportunities to get an early look at help-wanted ads, available the evening prior to publication, and to review the current business news, available in depth for the previous seven days.

The smorgasbord of non-job-related StarText features includes local news, features, travel services, entertainment, message boards, reference services, sports, an encyclopedia, stock and mutual fund prices, and more.

The *St. Louis Post-Dispatch* uses the *Star-Telegram* software for its system, PostLink. Beyond classified ads, available the previous evening, and the full local news report, PostLink offers an electronic bazaar of leisure-time and lifestyle features, including four hours on a national online service for a modest fee.

Access Atlanta, the service of the *Atlanta Journal and Constitution,* charges a small monthly fee for unlimited access to many features, including the classified ads.

An attractive feature of Access Atlanta is the "search" function. You avoid hours of searching for specific information merely by telling your computer the appropriate keywords, such as *environmental* or *sales.* The computer does the rest, zapping onto your screen every shred of data related to the keywords you select.

Selected Online Newspapers

Call your daily newspaper to discover whether it now offers—or plans to offer—electronic services to help the job seeker.

To get you started, here are telephone numbers for the newspapers noted in this chapter.

Albuquerque Tribune The Electronic Trib (505) 823-3664	*Hamilton Spectator* (Ontario) CompuSpec (416) 526-3303
Atlanta Journal and Constitution Access Atlanta (404) 526-5662	*Middlesex News* (Massachusetts) Fred the Computer (508) 626-3968
Beaumont (Texas) *Enterprise* EnterNet (409) 838-2821	*Newsday* Newsday Online (516) 843-2402
Charlotte Observer Connect:>Observer (704) 358-5249	*St. Louis Post-Dispatch* PostLink (314) 731-7678
Chicago Tribune Chicago Online (312) 222-4340	*Spokesman Review* S R Minerva (509) 459-5060
Fort Worth Star-Telegram StarText (817) 390-7154	

Chicago Online is produced by the Tribune Company, owner of the *Chicago Tribune*. The contents of the *Chicago Tribune* are made available online daily. Using keywords, you can search not only the service's extensive classified job listings, but the entire paper.

Beyond the newspaper online, Chicago Online offers a wide array of information, forums, and message boards for and about the Chicagoland area, all for a tiny basic cost per month.

A joint venture between the Tribune Company and America Online (described elsewhere in this chapter), the service is considered a "local area" of America Online. You get access to the full service of America Online when you subscribe to Chicago Online and vice versa.

In Canada, the evolution of online services can be followed by observing the changes in CompuSpec, the electronic system of The Hamilton Spectator. Initiated in 1986, the early features included some with news content, but the most popular offering has been the classified help-wanted ads.

In 1991, the ability to send electronic letters to the editor and a few interactive teleconferences (groups of people electronically chatting with each other) were added.

In 1993, the SPEC (Spectator Public Electronic Community) Link was launched. More than 30 new forums (special interest groups) were created to cover a wide range of topics from social issues to local economy concerns. The SPEC Link is a kind of community clue. Chiming in are business leaders, newspaper writers, patrons of public libraries, people with disabilities, and senior citizens, among thousands of other area residents.

Employment-related teleconferencing has proven to be of enduring interest. Discussions range from shared experiences of adult job seekers to students who talk about finding summer jobs.

The Hamilton Spectator gives this rationale for mounting a serious electronic effort: "We want to maintain our position as our community's information hub. Building a strong new network of people communicating with each other is good for newspapers and the communities they serve."

Mercury Center, an experiment of the *San Jose (California) Mercury News* is a fully searchable online service that includes help-wanted ads and access to all of the newspaper's stories since 1985, among other features. It was a new venture as this book was written.

Still more newspapers are operating some type of online service. Try the sources listed on page 119 for starters.

A business and library reference, *Newspapers Online*, published by BiblioData (P.O. Box 61, Needham Heights, MA 02194; 617-444-1154) is the directory that keeps track of more than 150 local, regional, national, and international daily newspapers that are on-line in full text. Classified ads usually are not included.

When you want to research company news, industry facts, or occupational information in more than one newspaper, particularly papers in a distant location, explore the use of online services that store newspapers. More than 100 newspapers worldwide offer access to their electronic libraries (files of stories—but not the classified ads—that have appeared in the newspaper over several years) through DataTimes, 14000 Quail Springs Parkway, Suite 450, Oklahoma City, OK 73134; (800) 642-2525. Look for this comprehensive service at large libraries or through independent information professionals.

DIALOG (described elsewhere in this chapter) also offers more than 50 newspapers' electronic libraries.

How can you use the rich resources in these newspapers? *Newspapers Online* editor Susanne Bjorner explains: "Suppose you are interested in finding a job in a particular geographic area, or in a particular industry. By doing a 'global' [all-encompassing] search in many newspapers at one time you can pull up lists of places to try.

"Our directory helps searchers know which sections of each newspaper would provide likely hunting grounds, and what they're called—business, money, metro, city, front page, and so on," Bjorner says.

Learning to use a wealth of newspapers vastly increases your career mobility, a key element in making sure your career remains on an upward track.

The electronic neighborhood is a reality in every community, observes John Granatino, director of electronic publishing at the *Providence (R.I.) Journal-Bulletin,* another newspaper now thinking electronic thoughts.

"As the rising percentage of household modem ownership and growing membership in national online services attest, more and more adults are going electronic to satisfy their needs for immediate information and immediate interaction with other people," Granatino says.

This includes individuals who are looking for new jobs immediately or who want to keep their antenna up for ongoing opportunity.

Prediction: Despite the heavy financial losses in electronic ventures during the 1980s, newspapers increasingly are seeing themselves as being in the business of communications rather than in the business of newspapers. Newspapers will become more important, not less important, in your job search.

THOUGHTS ON USING ONLINE HELP-WANTED ADS

Some estimates place the percentage of job openings that employers do *not* advertise at between 60 percent and 80 percent.

Even so, recruitment advertising is the single best source of identifying employers who have immediate job openings. The key reasons are described in the following sections.

More Job Advertising May Be Generated

"That single best source can get even better," says a recruiter in the Midwest. Why? "Money," answers the recruiter.

"You need people to prepare the ads, screen the replies, and send back letters of acknowledgment or regret—all that before other people even evaluate the real candidates. Electronics has become the magic wand of instant action. You can recruit with fewer people.

"Once the word about the new applicant tracking systems [described in the last chapter] trickles down, employers may be more willing to advertise their openings through both print and electronic media," the recruiter explains.

Job Ads Offer Immediate Employment

When it comes to putting rocket boosters under your job search campaign, print or electronic help-wanted ads are far superior to searching out jobs through slower-developing opportunities such as networks, employee referrals, walk-ins, public and private job services, and job fairs.

Despite the folklore we've all heard about phony help-wanted advertising designed merely to check the labor market—to see whether a current employee will reveal "disloyalty" by responding to the ad, or to accomplish a similarly devious design—the fact is the overwhelming majority of help-wanted ads are the real thing. They offer real jobs that are really available—and available *now*. Advertising has become too costly for employers to play games.

To put your efforts into perspective, bear this in mind: print media help-wanted ads remain the dominant recruiting source companies use. Study after study has shown this to be true.

Electronic help-wanted ads are joining print in the recruiting arsenals of employers, and you won't want to miss out on opportunities in an economy that is rapidly changing from one of a lot of hard-working people to one where there are fewer, smart-working people.

Old Ads Can Yield New Leads

Studying history can be a clue to the future. This is a theory job seekers use in looking back at old print classified help-wanted ads. By looking back eight to ten weeks, you might find a job not yet filled or one in which a false start was made by a new hire no longer with the company.

By looking back a year or two, you might discover a position from which the person hired has advanced or moved on, leaving a similar position open now. A downside to electronic job ads is usually that you can't look back. Most ads are deleted on a timely basis.

When you find an exception, an old electronic ad in your field, the same principle applies as for print ads: You've identified an employer who hires your kind of talent. Seize the initiative and apply.

MAKE ONLINE JOB ADS WORK FOR YOU

Match Replies and Requests

Once you find an electronic job listing to which you'd like to respond, study its wording and the priority of requirements. Work hard to make your cover letter and resume directly reflect the ad—yes, use the same keywords and synonyms for those keywords.

As a creative writing major says after "going electronic" in her job search, "Electronically speaking, I have learned not to be too clever. If they ask for 'excellent communication and interpersonal skills,' I tell them I have 'excellent communication and interpersonal skills.' I never knew how nice repetition could sound," she says with a grin.

Focus only on specific experiences sought by the employer, or on achievements you want to stand out. As much as possible, match each job requirement with a qualification you offer—documented by specific achievements.

Think in terms of key descriptors—college, major, grade point average, engineering specialty, language fluency, years of experience, and the like. Stress your accomplishments.

Avoid lumbering on with a laundry list of duties and responsibilities unrelated to the job at hand. (How to market your qualifications and respond to electronic job ads is discussed more fully in our companion book, *Electronic Resume Revolution*.)

Read between the Lines

Some people assume if something is new or technical, it must be right. In evaluating job listings on an electronic delivery system, it's best not to take anything at face value just because the information is coming to you in an unfamiliar format.

Just as you emphasize your strengths in a resume, advertisers stress their strong points in attracting your attention, whether by print or online delivery. They'd be fools not to showboat their positives.

An advertisement that emphasizes an "attractive plant" may mean the facilities are exceptionally pleasant, or it may be designed to distract your attention from the job's low pay.

An ad that highlights "excellent salary and benefits" may mean the employer is willing to pay for quality, or it may be deceptive in that it fails to include the fact that you're expected to put in 50-hour workweeks to receive great pay.

A larger than usual ad may suggest that the employer places a great degree of importance on the position, or that the employer runs a marginal workplace and needs to keep replacing people who leave.

Your hope is that what you see in an ad is what you get. The plant is gorgeous. The salary is superb. The employer appreciates good people.

You may get clues about the nature of the employer or the company culture from the way an electronic recruitment ad is worded and presented, but you can't be sure about an employer's perspective or agenda until you investigate further.

Stretch Your First Impressions

Don't prematurely assume that you are wrong for a job or that you don't want a job. Apply for anything in the neighborhood of what you want and can do, even if the pay is lower than your market value.

Why apply for a job that pays less than your market value? One reason is employers can't always find a mirror image of the employee they'd like to hire. They might be willing to upgrade a position for a senior person. Similarly, the employer may be willing to add another job for someone with potential but not enough experience.

Negotiate if Possible

Advertised job openings may give an impression that the salary offer is fixed, with no room for negotiation. In highly structured bureaucracies, salary negotiation is an uphill battle. To succeed you usually must get the position upgraded or move up the ladder to a higher position. In less structured settings, you may find employers more flexible than you may first think.

Try Out for Many Hats

Even if the job is not up to your standards, bear in mind what we discovered in the last chapter: *Once you're in a company's database, you can be called out for any job whose requirements match your qualifications—now or next year.*

It's a reasonable guess that companies advanced enough to advertise their job openings electronically probably are sophisticated enough to do applicant tracking electronically.

MORE POINTERS FOR READING ELECTRONIC HELP-WANTED ADS

Answer on First Ring

Respond at once to electronic ads that meet your qualifications. In responding to print help-wanted ads, it's often best to time your response to arrive a day or two after the big crush of mail. In viewing electronic ads, you can't be sure when the ad was first beamed out and you may be viewing it in the last days of its run.

Follow Up

After you respond to online ads, follow up. In addition to sending your resume (via modem, fax, or mail) to the person or address given in the ad, try to find out the name of the hiring manager. Mail or hand-deliver a copy of your resume to that manager, addressed by name and proper title.

Network to find a contact at the company and ask the contact to put in a good word for you with both the employment manager and the hiring manager. Start with electronics, and end with personal touch.

Search Resourcefully

Search large ads for "hidden" personnel requirements. Many big ads seek technical people, but they may be a small part of a company's work force. Ask about other openings to support the advertised jobs.

See through Titles

Thousands of job titles are common in the U.S. job market. One occupation may be known by a spectrum of titles, depending on the industry or the employer. An electrical engineer may be called a design engineer, a sales engineer, a test engineer, or an electronics research engineer—and these are only a few variations. When you're scrolling through the screens, remember a rose is a rose is a rose. Don't hesitate to apply even when you're not positive the job title listed is equivalent to the labels you use to describe the work you're capable of doing.

Manage Blind Ads

Blind ads, those that do not identify the employer, sometimes are used to avoid a huge response that could create a clerical monster. The easy-to-manage software may mean we'll be seeing fewer and fewer blind ads now that companies want resumes and can quickly send out acknowledgment letters.

Blind ads are also run to keep openings quiet, especially for jobs at a senior level.

When you spot an electronic blind ad you're tempted to answer, use caution to make sure your response doesn't wind up on your present employer's desk. Just as newspapers and trade journals offer blocking systems to bar any list of employers you specify from receiving your resume, so do operators of some online recruitment services.

Make sure you understand the confidentiality protection offered by the service you use. Learn exactly what the process offers and follow the instructions precisely.

If you live in fear of your employer's discovering you're restless, and you're not 100 percent certain that your resume is "safe," as a desperate resort you can use the third-person dodge for responding to a plum advertisement.

We don't recommend the third-person screen as something you should ordinarily try. But there are times when it's virtually the only move if you wish to respond to a choice blind ad.

In this stratagem, you ask a friend to respond for you. The friend contacts the employer: "I have an associate who appears to be an extraordinarily perfect match for your job requirements. My associate has asked that I serve as the liaison until mutual identities are established. Please telephone me at the following number and I will be pleased to put you in touch with my associate."

What does your friend say if the person who calls is, horrors, your boss?

Your friend truthfully mumbles that, upon reflection, the associate realizes the job is a mismatch, the salary is inadequate, the vacation requirement is three months, and thanks a lot, Mr. Boss, but no thanks.

Use Ads to Prospect

By staying current with the ads, you'll know which companies are expanding and hiring more personnel. When you see a company in a hiring mode, telephone to learn the name of the hiring manager in the area you'd like to work.

You may have trouble obtaining the appropriate name. Companies are wary about executive recruiters pirating their key personnel, or about job seekers bothering them with calls for employment. Be persistent; if you're quizzed, say it's personal and you're writing a letter, which is true.

Your letter to the hiring manager should outline your qualifications and offer convincing reasons for your wanting to work for the company. Request an appointment to talk about present or future job openings.

If you get in and nothing clicks, ask for referrals to the hiring manager's contacts in other companies.

Studies of how jobs are found show varying results, but it's commonly believed that a bare minimum of 20 percent of all available jobs are advertised. With 5 million jobs filled every year, that's quite a few. Even people who rely on networking as a primary job hunt strategy may miss out by failing to follow job ads.

Use Standard Job Descriptions

When you're thinking about responding to an ad but aren't quite sure you have a solid handle on the position's fine print, refer to a job description that closely matches the position.

Libraries have copies of job description books; a number are in electronic form, such as Job Scribe (see Chapter 7), a database of 3,000 authentic job descriptions from real companies for positions ranging from entry-level hires to senior executives.

Use Job Listings to Advance

Electronic surfing is useful in career management.

Suppose you think you might like to change your line of work but aren't sure what training and credentials you'll need. Recruitment ads to the rescue!

Read all the help-wanted ads, print and electronic. You may see, for instance, that employment calls for travel agents leave no doubt that a familiarity with computerized reservations systems is a must. You'll learn that office staff may be turned away if they do not know specific programs, such as Lotus or WordPerfect. You'll see that drafters must be literate in computer-assisted design.

If you seem to be missing a brick or two in your skills foundation, a crash seminar or a course at a community college or university can quickly build professional strength.

Even when you're not switching fields, you may want to refocus your campaign to fast-forward your job hunt. You may, for instance, find ten listings for entry-level marketers in environmental firms and only two for medical companies. A book on environmental studies can color your language green.

If you have any doubt about the kind of qualifications you need for the next step up the ladder, reading electronic help-wanted ads will be enlightening.

Summing up, the technology of advertising for help has come a long way from an 1870s ad in a frontier newspaper for people to get the mail from one place to another:

> Help Wanted. Pony Express Riders.
> Apply in person. High risk, low pay.
> Orphans preferred.

LIGHTS, CAMERA, JOBS!

If you'd rather watch or listen to recruitment advertising than read help-wanted ads, the telecommunications industry may be able to oblige.

Television and radio stations around the nation are creating programs to help people find work.

Typically, they receive good media reviews. They're novel and newsy and they hit the spot for a generation that grew up on television viewing.

Responding to job ads on television and radio may be free—you answer as though they are print recruitment ads. In some cases, a cost shifting takes place: the job seeker is forced to pay a few dollars to respond to the ad by calling a 900 telephone number.

It may be worth it to you to pay this slight administrative charge to receive a formal application form that will be read by a computer and evaluated against the job requisition.

Unfortunately for legitimate companies that view 900 numbers as profit centers, the shady and sleazy reputation of the early 900-number telephone industry may be a difficult obstacle to overcome in persuading job seekers to place their calls.

According to the Federal Trade Commission (FTC), you should be cautious of employment ads directing applicants to call 900 numbers.

In one paraphrased sample complaint to the Federal Trade Commission, a letter writer says:

> I saw an ad in the newspaper for a construction job. The ad said to dial an 800 toll-free number for an application. When I called, I was told to dial a 900 number to find out about job openings in my area. When I called that number, a recording told me to send a stamped, self-addressed envelope to have a job application mailed to me. All I got was a one-page generic job application and a 900-number charge for $39.00 on my telephone bill.

The FTC recently sued two companies advertising jobs in the United States using 900 numbers. These companies not only failed to disclose the cost of each call, which ranged between $10 and $18, but also they provided little, if any, information that would lead to a job.

Before you spend money to respond to a job ad, know what the 900-number call will cost. Reputable employment service companies will state the costs upfront. If you're ripped off with telephone charges for 900-number calls made to a fraudulent business, contact your telephone company immediately and ask that the charges be deleted.

To learn more, send for the free FTC booklets *Job Hunting: Should You Pay?* and *"900" Numbers*. They're available from the Federal Trade Commission, Public Reference, Washington, DC 20580.

We've alerted you to a *potential* for abuse. A number of classy operations have put in 900-number services. They range from the Consumers Union (the eternal foe of ripoffs) to the Catholic News Service.

"There is nothing inherently tarnished about 900 numbers," says a Consumers Union representative. And that's so. You are merely paying for information ranging from automobile resale values to movie reviews that factor in family values.

Quite apart from 900-number job scams, one more obstacle for 900 numbers as employment facilitators is the fact that applying for work is seen as an entitlement in this country.

Historically, American culture has not required people who are looking for jobs to pay a third-party fee merely to respond to employers who advertise open positions. This is true even when the third party says it is assisting the employer with the added service of "prescreening"—performing a computer match of the job requisition against the job seekers' applications before sending candidates to the employer. The entire cost of recruiting traditionally has fallen on the employer. For most Americans, the idea of paying to apply for work will take some mental reprogramming.

If the 900 pay-per-response idea becomes commonly accepted, the next question is: How will the working poor be able to afford to even look for work if it costs $4 or $5 a pop just to obtain an application?

Most of the jobs that are advertised on television and radio shows and require response through a 900-number system will not be near the lower rungs of the career ladder.

TV Show Examples

Here are a few examples of local television job shows.

Fox affiliate WTXF-TV in Philadelphia annually or biannually broadcasts "The Fox 29 Job Exchange," employment specials that include job opportunities as well as 30-second video resumes in which unemployed job seekers give glowing descriptions of their experience and abilities.

Job opportunities on WTXF-TV range from insurance agent to motorcycle mechanic, and chemist to tile installer. Those who market themselves through video resumes run the gamut from sales representative to office worker, and manufacturing director to department manager.

A statewide PBS affiliate, New Jersey Network, recently produced a 90-minute "Job Fair" to match employers and the jobless.

The show also featured video resumes of 25 job seekers selected by random drawing. Job opportunities, job search education, and financial coping skills, were highlighted.

Manning the New Jersey Network telephones, to connect callers with job openings, were placement counselors from the state's employment service.

The response to the "Job Fair" show was so positive the station has already aired "Job Watch," a follow-up series of nine half-hour programs featuring additional video resumes.

Most job shows are produced locally. One dramatic exception is "The Career Television Network," which broadcasts on the CNBC cable network one hour daily in a predawn time slot. The show offers an abundance of job features and job listings. Producers say one day the concept will expand to 24-hour programming over The Career Television Network's own cable service.

We'll stop with these few examples because, as you know, television and radio shows change frequently. What's hot today is what's not tomorrow. These several examples of how broadcasting is helping people to find jobs suggest yet another electronic avenue to explore.

MORE WAYS TO TAP TECHNOLOGY FOR JOB LEADS

As most people realize, the one-company career is all but obsolete. The days of "lifers" are over yesterday's hill.

If you do not want to be left behind yesterday's hill as well, you must know what kinds of jobs to go after and how to look for a new one when conditions change.

An advanced strategy to do this is roaring down the tracks like a great opportunity express. This spectacular new tool is the electronic employer database. Pay close attention.

5

Amazing New Electronic Employer Databases

For Dynamite Made-to-Order Job Leads, Nothing Beats These Information Age Tools

The previous chapter took us through electronic resources for recruitment advertising—actual advertised job openings that employers say they want to fill.

The other side of finding prospective employers is tapping into what is called the "hidden job market"—jobs that exist but are not advertised.

Computers can broaden your search arena by producing high-possibility target lists of people who can hire you.

Be honest. Would you turn down these opportunities to customize: A house you designed? A tailor-made suit? A world cruise where you chart the course? Neither would we, and that's what this chapter is about: how you can call the shots.

You have the power to write a wish list to describe your dream employer. You could jot down such criteria as:

- ▶ The kind of work you want to do.
- ▶ The kind of companies or organizations for which you want to work.
- ▶ The size of company you prefer.
- ▶ The company's financial stability.
- ▶ The location you prefer.

After you design a preferred profile of your next employer, you tell databases to search for these criteria and to print out a list of every potential employer that meets this profile. By using a computer, it's almost as easy as snapping your fingers.

What makes it possible is the 1990s' proliferation of electronic employer databases.

Outplacement and job search consultants have been using electronic databases since the 1980s, as a shortcut to the hidden job market.

But don't most people draw up job lists by using enormous print directories? If you want to struggle for hours to identify potential employers, you can still thumb through print directories, but electronic databases make it possible to quickly cut to the job chase. We're for that, aren't you?

DATABASES CLOSE UP

If you need a thumbnail definition of a database and a databank, here's the classic analogy. A database, a file of information, is like a chapter in a book. A databank is the book itself, consisting of many databases or "chapters."

In one sense, the database industry is at the chicken-or-egg stage of development. Most databases are too expensive to use on home computers, but developers are hesitant to invest huge sums of money to bring the prices down until there's greater demand. In time, there will be better balance; now, only a few databases for job hunters are definitely priced for home use.

Electronic employer databases come in various formats. The three most common are:

1. *Online*—Computer services can be either commercial or college-campus-operated; both types list information about employers. An online database is a one-way exchange, not an interactive system. It is designed to direct the job seeker in approaching a particular industry or profession.

Tips for Searching in a Database

Entering the world of information is like traveling to another planet—there's so much that has never been explored. If you've decided to go-it-alone on your research for a new job rather than enlist the help of an information broker, here are a few pointers. Author and information guru Sue Rugge (The Information Broker's Handbook, Windcrest/McGraw-Hill, 1992) has kindly provided us with tips to help smooth out what can be a bumpy road along your job search adventure.

1. Tapping this type of online database requires practice, skill, documentation, and training which, with many vendors, costs additional money, not to mention the sign-up fees at the start. In 1971, there were three databases on DIALOG. Today, there are about 6,000 databases on some 500 systems.

2. Your job is to get a job, not to become a researcher. There is no question, however, that learning about these resources may help you not only to find a job but to do an even better job when you get one.

3. The online information industry has a lot of weaknesses. If you approach this rich resource area as if it were a mature industry, you're likely to become disappointed, frustrated, and confused. It's still a wild and woolly place, particularly for new users. Keep your eyes open, and, until you feel you know what you're doing, keep your wallet close to your chest.

4. The real Achilles heel for the online information industry is inaccurate information. Most of us used to think that if something is in print, it has to be true. A small typo—a single letter—can be enough to throw off an entire search.

   For example, on one major service, there are 30,000 occurrences of the word "automobile" and another 300 for "automobiel". This is a problem for at least two reasons. First, if you are searching for articles on automobiles you will not find the references in which that word is misspelled. Second, if mistakes are made in the text, they can also be made in numerical data where detection is next to impossible.

5. Every database has different access codes even when several are on the same vendor system. You cannot search the databases without a road map—the vendor's "user documentation." Each database on DIALOG has chapters of documentation running between 30 and 50 pages, and each costs $15.

6. Every vendor system has a different language. Although the concepts of searching are the same throughout the industry, the means and commands for employing these concepts differ widely. You will

have to learn an entirely different "language" for each online system you wish to search.

There are things you can do on one system that simply can't be done on others. This is another reason to make sure you've not only selected the right database but are searching it on the most cost-effective system for your needs.

7. Don't always trust the update advisory provided by vendors. The advertised update schedule is not always met.

8. Time is money. Remember that most of these services make their money on your per-minute connect time. Who provides the greatest sources of revenue? Bumbling amateurs, who don't know what they're doing. For this and all the reasons above, a good argument can certainly be made for hiring a professional when you want to tap these powerful and sophisticated resources of information.

9. The above comments apply mainly to the large bibliographic and directory systems, but being forewarned will help you when searching the job offerings databases as well.

2. *CD-ROM* (Compact Disk-Read Only Memory)—An informational service can give details similar to those available with the online service, but they are recorded on a compact disk and can be read only by a CD-ROM player attached to a computer. CD-ROM is not interactive and cannot be updated by the user.

Most of the CD-ROM products mentioned in this chapter are also available online.

3. *Computer diskette*—Some database services issue their information on the popular 5^1/$_4$" or 3^1/$_2$" computer diskettes that nearly all PCs can read. The database service updates information on a periodic basis by simply issuing a new, inexpensive diskette.

TWO WAYS TO USE A DATABASE IN A JOB HUNT

The first way to use an employer database is to construct a target employer list.

The second way is to develop in-depth knowledge about specific companies and their personnel to use in job interviews. It is much easier to show how your qualifications fit a position's requirements when you know about the position and about the company.

For the best jobs, *advance research* is essential whether it comes from electronics, print, or people.

Because developing job leads and doing preinterview research overlap, we discuss them together in this chapter.

Basically, you are trying to find out such things as a firm's marketing methods, growth plans, research and development plans, product development or manufacturing plans, financial stability, employee benefits, quality as an employer, position in the industry, opportunity for advancement, reputation for keeping promises to employees, and so forth.

You want to know the names of the managers and executives, their biographies (maybe you went to the same school), and any hot news that may help you get hired.

Anticipate how helpful it could be if you were prepared to discuss all the business- and trade-press articles written about a company in the two years prior to going in for an interview with one of the company's executives. If you use the material gracefully, without sounding overprepared, such careful attention is impressive!

When you merely ask the computer to create a target list, the computer may identify, for example, 240 small companies and 39 large companies—with full contact information for managers of these companies—that meet the criteria you entered for location, industry, size, and type of organization.

Instead of calling into a bank of company switchboards too formidable to contemplate, you call up a database and ask your questions. In a few minutes—*voila!*—the computer spits out pages of the research needed to mount a first-class job marketing campaign.

If you're fuzzy about where you want to work, doing a customized target search is a waste of time and money. But if you know what you want, an electronic search is precision bombing that hits its target.

Let's look at another example. You can, for instance, establish target parameters and then go into the database and direct it to give you all the companies within a particular field that are located in your preferred geographic area and fit into your company-size boundaries of, say, $20 million to $100 million in annual sales.

Depending on how your search is structured, you'll have tons of information. If you've read other job hunt guides, you know how important it is to keep good records. You can use the sample format in Figure 5–1 for your top 20 or so job leads. Because you are unique and your search is unique, improve on this sample format by adding considerations that are important to you.

Organization _____

Address _____ City _____

State _____ Zip _____ Telephone _____ Fax/Modem _____

Key Personnel _____

Company Demographics

    Number of employees _____

    Quality of benefits _____

    Quality as an employer _____

    Opportunity for advancement _____

    Annual gross revenue (sales) _____

    Earnings _____

    Financial stability _____

    Facility locations _____

    Product(s) _____

    New product development _____

    Marketing methods _____

    Potential for expansion _____

    To where _____

Problem areas _____

Planned Personnel _____

    Positions I could fill _____

    Qualifications I have _____

_____

Figure 5–1 Employer Research Data Form

TIPS ON USING THE GREAT RESEARCH MACHINE

Using online databases isn't yet cheap, unless you live by the motto "Time is money."

If you're a new convert, you may be able to find a continuing education course or a community college to introduce you to the basics. When you're paying the bill, practice on inexpensive online databases, such as those on Knowledge Index on CompuServe, a service that operates at a discount at night and on weekends.

The cost of using the databases on CD-ROM or diskette varies widely. Some career counseling and outplacement firms offer them as part of their services. Many libraries carry employer databases. Some that you can buy for home use cost about the same as other software programs.

How can you identify the databases you want to search? Look through the list in the next section. No matter what your career field, chances are you'll find a database of interest. Don't be overwhelmed by the number of databases—they're enough to scramble anybody's calculator. Read through all the examples and mark those that are of particular interest for further exploration.

EXAMPLES OF ELECTRONIC EMPLOYER DATABASES

▶ *Barterbase:* Trustee Center for Professional Development, Hartwick College, Oneonta, NY 13820
   Telephone (607) 431-4425; Fax (607) 431-4318

This is an excellent database of companies that are good targets for liberal arts graduates.

Barterbase is maintained by a consortium of liberal arts colleges to help their graduates in the job search. Hartwick College in Oneonta, New York, took the lead in creating the consortium and serves as coordinator.

Each of the participating colleges contributes to the database. Hartwick College supports a database for private schools with teacher-fellowship programs. Hamilton College maintains a database of law firms that hire paralegals. Oberlin College is responsible for a database of publishers who hire editorial assistants.

Dickinson College's database is filled with international job opportunities. St. Lawrence University concentrates on environmental employers. Colby College lists those who hire in the performing arts and museums.

Students at member colleges can receive a computer disk with the relevant information, or they can turn on a modem-equipped computer, tap into the system, and directly request information online.

Because liberal arts majors often find it tough to land a job, Barterbase serves as a welcome source of information and a way to get to the so-called "hidden job market," including unadvertised jobs with smaller employers.

▶ **Business ASAP on InfoTrac:** Information Access Company, 362 Lakeside Drive, Foster City, CA 94404
    Telephone (800) 227-8431; Fax (415) 378-5369

This CD-ROM database contains the complete text of approximately 350 titles indexed in *Business Index, Business & Company Profile,* and *General BusinessFile.*
    Subjects covered in this service include business and industry, trade, management, and other business-related topics. Call the toll-free number for pricing information.

▶ **Business & Company ProFile:** on InfoTrac, Public Edition, Information Access Company, 362 Lakeside Drive, Foster City, CA 94404
    Telephone (800) 227-8431; Fax (415) 378-5369

Updated monthly, this CD-ROM database is a comprehensive source for business research on companies, products, markets, industries, economics, and management disciplines.
    The Business & Company ProFile indexes and abstracts about 700 business, management, and trade journals and links them to directory information for more than 140,000 private and public companies.
    This is a job seeker's dream: The service can spit out the full text of the news releases about companies carried on the PR Newswire. If you want to know what a company is proud of, this is a quick way to find out. Business and Company ProFile also contains indexing to four major newspapers.
    Another plus: You can keystroke in a city or state and retrieve the top 100 companies in that area, ranked by sales volume. Or you can search by industry or SIC (standard industrial code) to produce a list of companies within that industry, ranked by sales volume. All in all, a service not to miss.

▶ **Business America on CD-ROM:** American Business Information, Inc., 5711 South 86th Circle, P.O. Box 27347, Omaha, NE 68127
    Telephone (402) 593-4500; Fax (402) 331-1505

This library reference lists more than 10 million U.S. businesses, including retailers, wholesalers, service companies, and professional firms.
    The Business America On CD-ROM database includes key names, addresses, telephone numbers, and number of employees.

The job seeker can search with ease by type of business, state, county, and zip code, as well as telephone area code. The program comes on CD-ROM and online.

▶ *Business Dateline Ondisc, UMI:* 300 North Zeeb Road, Ann Arbor, MI 48106
       Telephone (800) 521-0600; Fax (313) 761-1203

This program is a CD-ROM version of Business Dateline online database. It contains the complete text of more than 350,000 articles from some 400 U.S. and Canadian regional business publications.

Business Dateline Ondisc covers news on local business leaders, companies, and products, as well as regional business trends.

This service carries subjects in electronics, retailing, real estate, service industries, hotels, restaurants, transportation, banks, financial institutions, and other industries.

Check with your library's reference desk.

▶ *Business Periodicals Index:* H. W. Wilson Company, 950 University Avenue, Bronx, NY 10452
       Telephone (800) 367-6770; Fax (718) 590-1617

This CD-ROM disk service contains more than 545,000 clips from articles and book reviews in some 345 business periodicals. Business Periodicals Index includes feature articles, interviews, biographical sketches of business leaders, book reviews, research developments, and new product reviews—loads of information for the job seeker wanting to do serious research on an industry or specific companies within an industry.

Some of the areas of business covered in this service include: accounting, advertising, banking, building and construction, chemical industry, communications, computers, economics, electronics, engineering, finance, food industry, government regulations, industrial relations, insurance, international business and management, marketing, and personnel administration.

Nuclear energy, occupational health and safety, oil and gas, public relations, publishing, real estate, and regulations of industry and transportation are also listed on Business Periodicals Index.

Look for this massive service at the reference desk in your library. The information is updated monthly, a big help when you need to know what's new.

▶ *Career Search:* 21 Highland Circle, Needham, MA 02194
Telephone (617) 449-0312; Fax (617) 449-4657

Career Search is a prime example of a way to trim endless hours in the library poring over enormous hard-copy directories of business and industry when you need to identify potential employers.

This electronic employer database is specifically designed for career transition centers at outplacement firms, college and graduate school placement offices, libraries, and other career services facilities. You can't just order it up on your own.

Career Search's nationwide database is reported to contain more than 200,000 companies of all sizes in 22 industrial categories.

The largest number of these are in the categories of manufacturing and high tech. Others include industries such as advertising, banking, hospitals, insurance, restaurants, and retail.

Career Search is easy to use. It gives on-screen help and lots of colorful icons and maps, which simplify choosing the criteria you want to use in a search. The selection criteria allow you to identify companies within desired geographic areas by city or zip code, as well as by size, specialty, and industry.

Once you identify companies, you can use the word processor of your choice and an automatic mail-merge feature to send customized cover letters and envelopes to corporate contacts.

The quality of data in a database is always a primary consideration. Career Search says its database is constantly updated and comes from publishers that specialize in specific market segments. Examples are Commerce Register for manufacturing, CorpTech for high technology, Gale Research for consulting, and R. L. Polk for banks.

Updates come out monthly, which means the information tends to be more current than in the printed industry directories by the same publishers.

▶ *CompuServe:* CompuServe, Inc., 5000 Arlington Centre Boulevard, P.O. Box 20212, Columbus, OH 43220
Telephone (800) 848-8199; Fax (614) 457-0348

CompuServe, a popular online information service that provides a wide range of less expensive database services, includes information retrieval on some databases that are likely to be useful in a job search.

Like other online services, CompuServe provides several news databases, such as Reuters, Associated Press, Business Wire, and *The Washington Post.* Full-text newspaper coverage includes 48 U.S.

newspapers online; issues go back nearly ten years. For company data, CompuServe's available databases include Coscreen, Disclosure, InvesText, and Standard & Poor's.

CompuServe has a low monthly subscription fee and its per-minute online charge for certain databases is inexpensive.

▶ *Corporate America:* Database America, 99 West Sheffield Avenue, Englewood, NJ 07631
    Telephone (800) 223-7777; Fax (201) 871-3649

This library reference database will be of special interest to marketing- and sales-oriented job seekers looking for room to grow.

Corporate America contains information on more than 1.4 million U.S. companies having sales greater than $1 million annually and work forces of more than 20 employees. Available on CD-ROM, it includes top executives by name and title, and is updated quarterly.

▶ *Corporate Jobs Outlook!:* Corporate Jobs Outlook, Inc., P.O. Drawer 100, Boerne, TX 78006
    Telephone (210) 755-8810; Fax (210) 755-2410

Corporate Jobs Outlook! is a standout database. It is unique in that it analyzes everything job seekers want to know about each company: key executives, sales figures, earnings, salary and benefit ratings, financial stability rating, industry outlook, company, outlook, and opportunity estimates.

It contains the complete text of *Corporate Jobs Outlook!*, a newsletter about career opportunities at leading corporations. The product covers employers from 45 areas of business, including aerospace, banking, computers, insurance, pharmaceuticals, and retailing. It is updated every two months and is available online from NewsNet Inc. and The Human Resource Information Network.

▶ *CorpTech:* Corporate Technology Information Services, Inc., 12 Alfred Street, Suite 200, Woburn, MA 01801
    Telephone (800) 333-8036; Fax (617) 932-6335

Available on diskette, the Corporate Technology Database—more commonly referred to as CorpTech—can be used to identify employers of high-tech personnel. It profiles more than 35,000 public and private U.S. corporations.

▶ *Dow Jones News/Retrieval:* Dow Jones & Company, Inc., P.O. Box 300, Princeton, NJ 08543
Telephone (800) 522-3567

This online database service is an electronic library of 1,750 business and financial information sources covering companies around the world. Included are *The Wall Street Journal,* Dow Jones News Service, and more than 1,400 other local, regional, national, and international industry publications.

Searches can be conducted by company name, stock symbol, industry and government codes, and executive name.

Job seekers can use the service to track the latest news on companies in which they are interested, research a company's finan- track record, get annual and quarterly reports, or even look up company telephone numbers and addresses and names of key executives.

In addition, career guidance information is available in the Career database. This service, updated daily, covers major national and international news stories since 1984. Online charges for the service are based on per-minute connection fees. Special low-price night-time (non-prime-time) rates are available.

▶ *Duns Million Dollar Disc:* Dun & Bradstreet Information Services, One Diamond Hill Road, Murray Hill, NJ 07974
Telephone (800) 526-0651; Fax (201) 605-6911

Duns Million Dollar Disc, a CD-ROM product of Dun & Bradstreet Information Services, is a library reference costing several thousand dollars annually.

This service is a widely used resource for employer information. It contains information on more than 200,000 public and private U.S. companies.

It covers the economic spectrum of commercial, industrial, and business establishments, giving full details on geographical locations. The big plus for job seekers is that this Dun & Bradstreet product on corporate giants lists the names and business background of top management personnel.

You can search by industry, location, and a number of other criteria. Updated quarterly, this is a "gold standard" of corporate databases.

▶ *General BusinessFile, Public Edition:* Information Access
Company, 362 Lakeside Drive, Foster City, CA 94404
Telephone (800) 227-8431; Fax (415) 378-5369

General BusinessFile is a CD-ROM product that bills itself as the
only fully integrated database covering all aspects of business, management, company, and industry information.

It consolidates the most respected investment reports available
and corporate profiles of public and (hard to find) private companies. It also includes wide-ranging, current business news from
trade, industry, and management journals and newspapers.

Designed specifically to meet the needs of library users, General BusinessFile provides one-stop research on job hunting strategies, as well as other subjects such as investments, local and regional
economic trends, consumer surveys, small business management,
and new technologies and products.

Topics available for research are international trade, mergers
and acquisitions, key industry and market trends, management the-
ories, and general economics. The service is updated monthly.

▶ *Hoover's Handbooks:* Reference Press, Inc., 6448 Highway 290-E,
Suite E-104, Austin, TX 78723
Telephone (512) 454-7778; Fax (512) 454-9401

This low-cost database contains information on 1,000 of the largest,
most influential, and fastest growing companies. It provides company overviews and histories, lists competing companies, and gives
the names, addresses, and telephone/fax numbers of key personnel.

Portions of the Hoover's Handbook database are available on
CD-ROM for Sony's Data Discman and MMCD players for less than
$40 and $60 respectively. Hoover's Handbooks are also available online through Lexis/Nexis and America Online.

▶ *Investext on InfoTrac:* Information Access Company, 362 Lakeside
Drive, Foster City, CA 94404
Telephone (800) 227-8431; Fax (415) 378-5369

This service contains indexing or full text of some 30,000 company/in-
dustry reports. This covers over 11,000 U.S. and international companies in 53 industries. The data come from 270 of the world's leading
investment banks, brokerage firms, and consulting and research firms.

Investext can be used to analyze a company's line(s) of business, check a company's financial health, and locate current and his-
torical financial information.

▶ *Lexis/Nexis:* Mead Data Central, Inc., P.O. Box 933, Dayton, OH 45401
  Telephone (800) 227-4908; Fax (513) 865-6909

The Lexis online financial service contains such company data as annual reports and investment analyst research reports.

The Nexis online service contains a broader range of databases, including Asia/Pacific, banking, campaign news, computers, companies, consumer goods, energy, entertainment, environment, Europe, insurance, medicine, patents, and sports.

Nexis carries *The New York Times* and other newspapers. The user can search for data in newspapers individually, as a group, or in a customized package.

Prices vary, depending on service selected. There is a monthly subscription fee plus a per-minute connection charge. This service may be available at your library.

▶ *Martindale-Hubbell:* Reed Reference Publishing Company, 121 Chanlon Road, New Providence, NJ 07974
  Telephone (800) 526-4902; Fax (908) 464-3553

Lawyers can cruise the Martindale-Hubbell Law Directory database to identify potential employers of legal counsel. Identified are more than 800,000 lawyers and law firms, in excess of 1,000 corporate law departments, and 2,000 services and suppliers to the legal profession worldwide.

This employer database, available in CD-ROM and online through the Lexis/Nexis services, ideally illustrates services tailored for specific occupations. In this case, lawyers can search by state, county, city, name of firm, name of client, name of attorney, college, college year, law school, law school year, legal services, and much more.

The service, which is usually available at law libraries, university libraries, and large public libraries, is updated semiannually on CD-ROM and throughout the year on Lexis/Nexis. (See Lexis/Nexis database service above.)

▶ *Moody's Bank & Finance Disc:* Moody's Investors Services, Inc., 99 Church Street, New York, NY 10007
  Telephone (800) 342-5647; Fax (212) 553-4700

For job seekers looking for positions in banks, savings and loans, and other financial berths, Moody's Bank & Finance Disc is packed with solid information on U.S. financial institutions. The data include company history and business description for thousands of entities. The product is offered on CD-ROM disk.

Updated quarterly, the timely information corresponds to the *Moody's Bank & Finance Manual*.

▶ ***Moody's Industrial Disc:*** Moody's Investors Services, Inc., 99 Church Street, New York, NY 10007
Telephone (800) 342-5647; Fax (212) 553-4700

Moody's Industrial Disc offers business information on nearly 2,000 industrial corporations, and includes company history and description. The database comes on a CD-ROM disk and is updated quarterly. It corresponds to the *Moody's Industrial Manual*.

Both of these Moody disks can be accessed by using MoodEASE software, available from Moody's Investors Services Inc. Call the company for details.

▶ ***S&P Corporations:*** Standard & Poor's Corporation, 25 Broadway, New York, NY 10004
Telephone (212) 208-8300; Fax (212) 412-0498

Another major database that may be available through a library's business reference desk, S&P Corporations is a comprehensive product that contains descriptive details and financial data on U.S. corporations in three files:

1. Executives holds biographical profiles of more than 70,000 key personnel.
2. Private Companies profiles more than 45,000 leading private U.S. corporations.
3. Public Companies tallies 12,000 publicly traded companies.

S&P Corporations is available as a CD-ROM disk through Dialog Information Services (Dialog OnDisc).

▶ ***Ultimate Job Finder:*** Planning/Communications, 7215 Oak Avenue, River Forest, IL 60305
Telephone (800) 829-5220; Fax (708) 366-5280

This extensive, pleasant-to-use database of job leads is a compilation of three popular guidebooks in the Job Finder series: *Professional's Private Sector Job Finder, Non-Profit's Job Finder,* and *Government Job Finder.* All are published by Planning/Communications.

The reasonably priced database, available on both sizes of diskettes, reports on more than 4,700 sources that can lead you to hundreds of thousands of job vacancies. Sources include many job hotlines, job-matching services, specialty and trade periodicals, and computerized job or resume databases.

Career fields available in the Ultimate Job Finder's software cover the waterfront, from education, environment, health care, social services, and teaching to engineering, foundations, higher education, legal services, music and dance, and school administration.

This annually updated product also includes descriptions of salary surveys and job search advice on writing cover letters and resumes and on interviewing.

One way to use the Ultimate Job Finder is to key in an occupation and watch a detailed description of every job source for that career area flash on the screen. You can browse through the descriptions and print out those you want.

The Ultimate Job Finder sparkles on government search assignments, listing what is probably the most complete compendium of resources for government jobs at local, state, and federal levels.

▶ *Companies International:* Gale Research, Inc., 835 Penobscot Building, Detroit, MI 48226
  Telephone (800) 347-4253; Fax (313) 961-6815

Companies International is another CD-ROM you should look for at a library reference desk. This annual service profiles more than 135,000 public and private U.S. companies including difficult-to-track, privately-held firms. Top executives are listed, as well as the number of employees, revenue, and industry.

This CD-ROM corresponds to the five-volume printed *Ward's Business Directory of U.S. Private & Public Companies* and to the *World Trade Centers Association World Business Directory.*

ELECTRONIC RESEARCH SERVICE BUREAUS

Perhaps now you appreciate the big boost an electronic search can give your career. But let's face it: Not all of us are crazy about using computers for anything. As one wag says, "If builders built buildings the way programmers write programs, then the first woodpecker that came along would destroy civilization."

If you dread the thought of firing up a computer and becoming an instant expert on information search, why not hire an electronic researcher to do the computer legwork for you?

Electronic researchers are combination computer and research whizzes who can produce highly accurate job lead lists.

Because job search electronic research is a fairly new occupation, you may need to call around and check backgrounds to find the best researcher for you.

You may be able to locate job search electronic researchers—also called job market information consultants—by asking at your library or college career center.

Hiring a job search electronic researcher will cost you between about $65 to $150 an hour. Some charge a minimum fee of $500 or more. Often, you won't have to spend more than $100 to $200 for a customized list of target companies and recruiters.

It may sound expensive but there is a learning curve for each database, and the wrong keystroke with an online system can be costly because most online services charge by the minute.

If you need more justification in your desire to avoid computers, one information consultant points out, "Your goal is to land a job, not learn how to research."

Before you put money on the electronic researcher's table, observe these common sense rules:

1. Check references of former clients. Call and ask whether the data supplied by the electronic researcher were relatively valid and current—or whether they were filled with information so out-of-date it was easily confused with bleu cheese.

2. Check whether any complaints were filed with the Better Business Bureau or the state consumer protection office.

3. Ask the researchers for specifics on the data you're buying. What databases are used? How large are they? How often are they updated? Unless you're in an obscure occupation, a benchmark is that your search should be conducted in databases of more than 200,000 companies.

4. Get a clear understanding *in writing* of what it will cost you.

5. Be clear in your mind about one thing: You are not buying a list of companies with job openings. The electronic researchers have no way of knowing who is hiring and who is not. They are providing you with a list of *prospective* employers or recruiters who may or may not be able to advance your job search. That's all. For this reason, it's difficult to establish a meaningful refund policy.

6. Find out how you will receive the data—paper, fax, diskette, modem. Once a researcher has the raw material to shape your search, the data can be organized in many ways—by geographic

location, industry ranking, sales, number of employees, years in business, and so forth.

Some electronic research service bureaus, for an additional charge, will create mailing packages of letters (from letters you compose), envelopes, or labels.

Suppose you don't get more than ten really good leads. Should you get a refund because you didn't get twenty really good leads? Or hundreds of really good leads? You'll have to think about this and decide what information you must receive to make your investment worthwhile.

As examples, here are two firms that will handle your action in finding the employers or recruiters who deal in your type of job.

▶ *Pro/File Research:* P.O. Box 602, Flourtown, PA 19031
   Telephone (215) 643-3411; Fax (215) 643-3626

This electronic research service bureau is a prime example of the new breed of specialists who encourage you to "Leave the searching to us." The firm can identify both companies and executive recruiting firms of interest—as specified by you. In addition to individuals, career counselors often call Pro/File Research to prepare job lead packages for their clients.

A new and interesting feature is a service to assist the "trailing" spouse of a transferred employee.

When a spouse is transferred by a company, the employer usually offers assistance with real estate, moving expenses, and travel, but some firms add a program of spousal job placement assistance.

Pro/File Research can access a database of some 10 million employers and 2,200 executive recruiters to identify all the possible employers in the requested parameters within a designated geographic area.

In a recent search, a spouse wanted a list of manufacturers of fabricated metal products with at least 200 employees, located in an area of eastern Massachusetts and northern Rhode Island that was within commuting distance from the spouse's new home.

The Pro/File Research package turned up 91 companies. We don't know whether a job jackpot was the result—most electronic researchers never hear the end of the story unless they make a special effort to follow up. Most of the 91 companies won't pan out, but several could be perfect job leads. Can you imagine the time saved by electronic search? Impressive!

As another plus for job seekers, Pro/File Research offers a laser-printed envelope service that matches the addresses on the list of

Electronic Research to the Rescue

For the middle-aged executive who spends years nurturing a career only to see it come crashing down, starting-over information bestowed by an electronic research bureau can be like a gift from on high.

Stephen Shea was the president and owner of a successful Philadelphia grain-processing company that produced flour for the snack food industry.

He spent ten years developing his business, but suddenly it all came tumbling down when the Federal Deposit Insurance Corporation (FDIC) seized the bank supplying his corporate line of credit and all of his company's bank accounts.

The FDIC immediately called the loan on Shea's line of credit and seized all the cash assets he had in the bank. Shea says his company's checks bounced all over the place.

In a short period of time, Shea lost his company and had to begin over again. He went to an executive career counseling firm to reconstruct his career and life.

"I spent about six months looking for either another company to buy, or to find a job with a company who needed my expertise," recalls Shea. "The career counseling firm I signed with provided me with a job lead package from Pro/File Research, an electronics research bureau in Flourtown, Pennsylvania.

"Pro/File took the parameters [specifications] of the search for companies that might use my talents, which are located in geographic areas I would consider moving to," says Shea. "The search also included data on the products these companies produce and each company's financial status."

In a matter of a few days, Shea says, he was provided with a good-size list of companies and their profiles from three geographic areas. He used the list to begin his campaign.

"Pro/File Research laid out all of this information so that I could approach these companies directly," Shea explains. "There was no information or indication provided as to whether or not any of these companies were or would be hiring."

Shea says his personal experiences with the career counseling firm are typical.

"I paid a fee, but I did 90 percent of the actual job search preparation myself," he explains. "They [the career counseling firm] lined up and organized some things to help with my job search."

After receiving the lists of companies fitting his requirements, Shea sent a resume and cover letter to those companies that met his criteria. Shea says this part of the job search is "all one-way." By that he means

he had no idea whether any of the companies he wrote to would respond or would even be interested in talking to him.

At least one was interested—and it only takes one.

Today, Shea remains in the Philadelphia area working for a small
food processor he connected with through the electronic job lead
package provided by Pro/File Research. He not only has an option to
buy the company, but, if things don't work out, he has a standing job
offer from a large Connecticut food processor—another of the companies Pro/File Research identified for him.

"I got lucky," Shea concludes. "I found a company who needed
the expertise I have, and one I wanted to work with. For me, electronic
research paid off."

recruiters and target companies, as well as cover letters that use the
job seeker's text.

You advise this service what sort of employer you're looking for
and where you'd like to locate, and you provide the text for the communications. Next, all you do is stuff the printed envelopes that the
service has addressed with your tailor-made letters to the companies you selected, lick the stamps, and drop the stamped envelopes
into the mail. Then pray that if you don't strike oil with an immediate opening, the companies use applicant tracking systems that will
cherish and save your resumes.

▶ *InfoWorks:* 2498 Rawson Street, Oakland, CA 94601
     Telephones (800) 437-9303 or (510) 536-3208; Fax (510) 536-0780

Deborah Bryant, President of InfoWorks, prepares job lead packages
and preinterview briefs, as well as other specialized searches such as
the market rate for a position. The typical cost to each client is between $150 and $225.

This employment research firm serves more than jobless
clients. Employed people with a wandering eye turn to Bryant for
help either because they have no time to compile the research or because they're afraid the boss will catch them doing it on company
time.

Here are the key points as Bryant describes them:

▶ InfoWorks is a research firm for job seekers. It is not a placement
    or an employment firm. InfoWorks supplies the information job
    seekers need to effectively market themselves: preinterview

briefs, salary surveys, prospect lists, relocation assistance reports, job outlook summaries, and more.

▶ Online databases are used on job seekers' behalf to search newspapers anywhere in the United States, trade and professional literature, business directory files, financial reporting files, and more. Telephone research is added to obtain unpublished or ultra-current data.

▶ InfoWorks answers job seekers' questions, from the routine—such as a business credit profile to determine whether a company is solvent—to the extraordinary—such as a report on the use of nutritionists to handle food accounts at public relations firms.

Bryant explains why looking at a company's financial figures prior to an interview, even when you're not applying for a job in accounting or financial management, is important.

"Financial figures and statistics such as annual sales reflect on a company's ability to hire, promote, and retain employees. When possible, look for trends by comparing company figures over the last three to five years. How are they doing? Employment research should pull up this data for you," Bryant says.

As word of employment electronic researching spreads, job seekers will use it to sniff out job opportunities and carefully target

---

Facts in a Flash

Ellen Jason (a fictitious name for a composite of several people) was called for an interview at a large San Francisco advertising agency. Jason was ecstatic, ten feet off the ground—it was her dream job.

She came down to earth quickly when she realized that the interview was set for Tuesday morning and this was Friday at 11 A.M. How could she whip herself into shape in time?

Turning to InfoWorks, Jason ordered a preinterview brief. By Saturday at 2 P.M., Jason had a package of information on the advertising firm, from sample press releases and financial data to information on the names of top executives and print articles about the ad agency. She had some data about the firm's major accounts, their primary competitors, and the trends in the advertising industry. She knew the going rate for this position in the San Francisco area.

Ellen Jason had all she needed to walk into that job interview with confidence and show how she and the job were a good match. She was ready to bargain to be paid what she was worth.

---

prospective employers for the same reasons that businesses use market intelligence to keep tabs on competitors.

Bryant's motto for InfoWorks is increasingly true for job seekers: "Because What You Don't Know Will Hurt You."

INFORMATION BROKERS WITH JOB SEARCH EXPERIENCE

In addition to electronic research service bureaus whose employees do nothing but job search, here are selected information brokers across the nation who have experience preparing job lead lists and doing literature search (researching information from articles, annual reports, and other sources for interviews).

Although this is not a complete list, we have compiled it with the aid of reliable information professionals. Prices depend on many factors, so confirm costs in advance of a search with each information broker.

Berinstein Research
Paula Berinstein
P.O. Box 1305
Woodland Hills, CA 91365
Telephone (818) 704-6460
Fax (818) 704-1590

Susanne Bjorner
Bjorner & Associates
7 Tamarack Lane
Woodbury, CT 06798
Telephone (203) 263-4759
Fax (203) 263-0278

Burwell Enterprises
Helen Burwell
3724 F.M. 1960 West No. 214
Houston, TX 77068
Telephone (713) 537-9051
Fax (713) 537-8332

Cooper Heller Research
Linda Cooper
622 South 42nd Street
Philadelphia, PA 19104
Telephone (215) 823-5490
Fax (215) 823-5493

Corporate Fact Finders
Sharon Dean
884 Westtown Road
West Chester, PA 19382
Telephones (800) 220-3228;
   (215) 431-3708
Fax (215) 431-0674

Datasearch
Sue Feldman
170 Lexington Drive
Ithaca, NY 14850
Telephone (607) 257-0937

Desktop Information
Steve McIntosh
32 W. Anapamu, No. 200
Santa Barbara, CA 93101
Telephone (805) 963-4095
Fax (805) 564-4878

F1 Services
Chris Dobson
3141 Hood Street
Dallas, TX 75219
Telephone (214) 528-9895
Fax (214) 528-9819

Fluxdata Research Services
Tim Green
407 North Main Street
London, OH 43140
Telephone (614) 852-0202
Fax (614) 852-0344

InfoLink
Janet Gotkin
31 Albany Post Road
Montrose, NY 10548
Telephone (914) 736-1565
Fax (914) 736-3806

Information Express
Oksana Carlson
2266 North Prospect Avenue
No. 314
Milwaukee, WI 53202
Telephone (414) 272-5250

Joat Information
Alvin Kimble
244 East 46th Street
New York, NY 10017
Telephone (212) 370-9589

Library Specialists, Inc.
Jane Miller
1000 Johnson Ferry Road,
No. D105
Marietta, GA 30067
Telephone (404) 578-6200
Fax (404) 578-6263

MarketingBase
Amelia Kassel
1364 Kathy Lane
Sebastopol, CA 95472
Telephone (800) 544-5924
Telephone (707) 829-9421
Fax (707) 823-2713

Martin Goffman Associates
Dr. Martin Goffman
3 Dellview Drive
Edison, NJ 08820
Telephone (908) 549-5433
Fax (908) 906-1687

Mercury Information Services
Larry Krumenaker
P.O. Box 191
Hillsdale, NJ 07642
Telephone (201) 358-9560
Fax (201) 358-9372

Notes Unlimited
Cliff Williams
14301 Swan Lane
Gulfport, MS 39503
Telephone (601) 832-8731
Fax (601) 831-3045

Ojala Associates
Marydee Ojala
P.O. Box 770
Park City, UT 84060
Telephone (801) 649-7652
Fax (801) 649-8362

Online Research
John Witmer
111 Rainbows End
Anderson, SC 29624
Telephone (803) 375-1512
Fax (803) 375-1408

Silver Birch Enterprises
Stanley D. Moreo
1310 Maple Avenue, No. 3C
Evanston, IL 60201
Telephone (708) 864-4494
Fax (708) 866-8884

The Information Consultancy
Mary Park
308 Tunbridge Road
Baltimore, MD 21212
Telephone (410) 532-7275
Fax (410) 433-8793

The Rugge Group
Jim Hydock
2670 Mountain Gate Way
Oakland, CA 94611
Telephone (510) 530-3635
Fax (510) 530-3325

YOUR VISION OF THE FUTURE

Wondrous, isn't it—how the new electronic employer databases can produce customized products for you, to your specifications?

These opportunities come just in the nick of time for the ambitious manager and professional competing in a new information-technology-driven global marketplace.

Take your cue from a favorite old French saying that admonishes would-be travelers to chart their course before setting out:

What! No star, and you are going out to sea?
Marching, and you have no music?
Traveling, and you have no map?

Speaking collectively of the electronic databases just described: THIS is your map!

6

The Computerized Job Interview

When Computers Greet You at the Door, Take Your Application, and Test Your Skills

In previous chapters, we focused on the matchmaking aspects of job search—how people and jobs find each other. In this chapter, we focus on what happens after they find each other.

Interviewing often is done in two basic stages: screening and selection. Human resource specialists typically do the screening, making sure that applicants are qualified for the position in question. Managers to whom the new employee would report usually do the selection interviews.

This chapter will make you aware of how the functions involved in the screening interview—which may or may not include filling out application forms and having your skills and integrity tested—are circling around computers.

Two basic models exist. The first begins with human contact, moving to a computer interview; the second begins with a computer application, moving to human contact. Skill and integrity testing can be a part of either model.

Imagine this: You see a help-wanted ad, respond, are invited to fill out an application form and then are asked to return the next morning for a job interview. So far, so good—a routine approach.

When you return the following morning, the receptionist says, "Follow me," and you do, expecting to be greeted by a smiling interviewer. Your mouth is open to say "Nice office" when you notice that the receptionist has escorted you to an empty room. There's nothing, and no one, in it—except for a computer terminal sitting on a stand. The computer isn't smiling, and it couldn't care less about your impression of the decor.

Why are you and the terminal being left alone in the room? The receptionist explains. Your initial screening interview, the first cut that separates the good bets from the near misses, will be conducted by a computer! A bit different—not so routine an approach.

Has hiring come to this? Are people going to be judged by machines? No, but for certain jobs in some corporations, computers are supplementing the human resource staff by giving human interviewers a hand. Computers help, but, thank heavens, people still hire people.

Here's what happens during a typical computer-assisted interview.

You sit at a terminal and work through a series of some 50 to 100 multiple-choice questions about employment history, job qualifications, and general background.

Once you're finished, you'll be asked to wait a few minutes before you have the opportunity to speak with a human interviewer. What you may not realize is that the job application you filled out yesterday was fed into a computer. It is compared to a printout of data obtained from the computerized interview you just completed. Do the answers look as though they came from the same person? Are there glaring differences? An evaluation is made.

A human interviewer checks the evaluation. It shows not only the answers you gave, but which questions took you an unusually long time to answer. The evaluation red-flags areas of concern the human interviewer should probe. To the question "Is it okay to take damaged goods?", for example, the interviewer will no doubt want to pursue a response of "It depends."

As we noted, the computerized interview includes questions you previously answered on the application form; it may ask the same questions in different ways to see whether your answers match.

Suppose on your application you say you are a high school graduate, but in the computer interview you add that you have "some college." The interviewer will want to know why you gave different answers. Or, in the interview, one question asks about standing on your feet for prolonged time spans and you say it will aggravate a back problem, but in answering another question, you say it will not be a problem to lift 30-pound boxes. The interviewer will certainly want to probe this disparity.

HOW HAS COMPUTER-ASSISTED INTERVIEWING HELD UP?

Since 1978, when the first person to be interviewed by a computer for a job made history at Corbin Ltd., a sewing factory in Huntington, West Virginia, more than 6 million job applicants have followed in her keystrokes.

The Greentree Computer-Assisted Employment Interview was the first of its kind and has evolved over a 15-year history to its present prominence.

The majority of users of this system—now operated by its developer, Brooks Mitchell, PhD, president of Aspen Tree Software, Inc.—are hotels and retailers, hospitals, teleprocessing operators, and many other employers who hire large volumes of people.

We find this to be a relatively fair interviewing method because everyone is asked the same questions in the same way, and most of the questions dig beneath the surface for attitudes and personal traits. You can win by being consistent and by not hesitating over questions of honesty and ethics.

Most corporate users of computer-assisted employment interviews report improvements in the personnel selection process in such areas as worker turnover, absenteeism, theft, and productivity. A consensus among users reportedly points to an overall improvement in the quality of the employee hired because the computer helps decision makers overcome problems inherent in the traditional job interview. These problems include judgment factors among interviewers and the consistency of their questions.

What are we talking about here, a kind of pilot error syndrome among interviewers? Possibly. Research indicates disadvantages of the human-to-human interview do exist. Interviewers' errors include: forgetting to ask important questions, talking too much, being reluctant to ask sensitive questions, forming unjustified negative first impressions, obtaining unreliable information that makes an applicant feel unfairly judged, and using interview data ineffectively.

By contrast, a computer-assisted employment interview, say its proponents, creates a good interview because it incorporates many of the skills and experiences of seasoned interviewers and avoids the recognizable pitfalls of human-to-human interviews.

Advocates of computer interviewing say computers present job applicants with questions that, although they are multiple-choice, do require reflection. The computer is programmed to spot inconsistent or problematic answers.

Here's a sampling of computer interview questions:

1. George, if you were given a supervisory position, how would you evaluate your chances for success?

    A. Very poor; this would not be a good job for me.

    B. Poor; I don't think I would perform well.

    C. Fair; I think I could do an adequate job.

    D. Good; I think I would perform above average.

    E. Excellent; I think I would be highly successful.

    F. I am not sure how I would perform.

2. George, how would you rate your performance at the Acme Brick Company?

    A. Very poor.

    B. Poor.

    C. Fair.

    D. Good.

    E. Excellent.

    F. I'm not sure.

3. George, could we have your permission to contact Sam Katz [George's previous supervisor] to see how he would rate your job performance at the Acme Brick Company?

    A. Yes.

    B. Possibly.

    C. No.

Greentree experts explain that people would rather talk to a computer than a person, especially in sensitive subject areas. Let that piece of information be a clue: Don't tell a computer anything you would not reveal to a human interviewer. The computer won't keep your secrets.

Why do people respond more honestly to a computer than to a human interviewer? Partly because the computer is a peerless interviewer—ageless and sexless—and thus less suspect and threatening than a human interviewer. Job hunters may not feel embarrassed to respond to a computer because they know it won't be shocked or disappointed by their response. One university study reveals that when applicants admit to a computer the amount of alcohol they put away, it is higher than the amount they describe to a human interviewer.

The following information frequently is contained in the computer-generated report human interviewers receive before the face-to-face meeting:

▶ *Response summary.* This item summarizes the job applicant's responses and categorizes them under such major headings as work history and life experience.

▶ *Contradictory responses.* The applicant may have indicated he or she was terminated from the most recent job because of poor attendance; at a later point in the interview, he or she may indicate that an outstanding recommendation was received from a former employer.

▶ *Late responses.* When an applicant takes longer than average (as measured by the applicant's own average time of response) to answer, responses to those questions are itemized.

▶ *Potential problems.* This category identifies problem answers in areas predetermined by the employer. A response indicating the applicant intends to remain on the job for less than a year would be clearly highlighted for the interviewer as a problem response.

▶ *Suggested questions for interviewer.* These questions, which are pre-constructed by the employer, are chosen for each applicant based on his or her responses to the multiple-choice questions. For example, the computer may prompt the interviewer to ask, "George, you mentioned that you feel a previous employer would rate your performance as average. Why don't you feel it would be higher?" This feature ensures additional control and consistency of the job interview.

From the hiring company's viewpoint, the computer-assisted interviewing process makes sense because it can give the interviewer information that may not otherwise be obtained.

From the job seeker's side of the process, it is necessary to be far better prepared for an interview than ever before. You must understand how the process works—and how it can work against you. You are ahead when you understand some of the gritty psychology behind the structure of the questions.

A number of Fortune 1000 companies are adding the computer-assisted interviewing process to their human resource departments: Marriott Hotels, Exxon, American Express, Neiman Marcus, American General Insurance, General Tire, Corning Glass, and Kaiser Permanente are among those using this innovative technique.

To learn more about The Greentree Computer-Assisted Employment Interview, contact Aspen Tree Software, Inc., 1159 Granito, Laramie, WY 82070; Telephone (307) 721-5888; Fax (307) 721-2135.

Dovetail is another well regarded and comprehensive computerized interviewing program that major companies are using to screen job applicants. Dovetail is a software package marketed by The Dovetail Group in Atlanta.

The Dovetail Computer Interview program is multi-faceted and many-splendored; it is designed to assist the face-to-face human interviewer with a highly focused and structured interview. Dovetail contains assessment and profiling features.

(Human resource readers will want to know that, like some of the programs described in Chapter 3, Dovetail is a full-service HR resource, offering an applicant tracking capability, a database search feature, automatic letter-writing power, plus other useful personnel office tools. Dovetail departs from other computerized interview programs in that it allows the human resource specialist to compare every applicant to a company-specific database of employees in various profiles—low turnover, high performance, and so on. This feature further guides the face-to-face interviewer through detailed and intense discussions.)

From the job applicant's standpoint, the use of Dovetail's computerized programs suggest greater scrutiny is being given to your quest for the position. All the "t's" are being crossed and all the "i's" dotted.

From the human resource specialist's standpoint, Dovetail is designed to give a kind of infrared scope to use in the dark areas of choosing the best person for the job.

Dovetail Software can be reached at 11 Piedmont Center, Suite 810, Atlanta, GA 30305; Telephone (800) 421-2341; Fax (404) 262-9167.

WHEN APPLYING FOR A JOB IS LIKE GETTING CASH AT AN ATM

Remember when you had to wait in line to see a teller to get cash out of your bank? And remember how you learned to save time when withdrawing cash by learning to follow the menus on an automatic teller machine (ATM)?

Well, now you can do something like that in applying for a job. As an example, a large bank that hires 50 new people on the average each week, has installed the Restrac Kiosk system to provide "job applications on demand." It's like an ATM for job applications.

The kiosks are used to accept applications from walk-in applicants. Job seekers sit in front of a computer and fill out their applications.

Suppose you are the applicant. You are asked a question and given space to keyboard the answer. Succeeding questions are based on your answers to previous questions, just like an ATM asks you different questions after you tell it whether you are there to make a deposit or a withdrawal. Finished? You're asked to review your application and okay it. When you do, your application is whisked away into the bank's applicant tracking system.

It may take a little getting used to. For those of you who appreciate teller machines, you'll love it right off the bat. Especially if your handwriting is not easily read.

The bank's Restrac Kiosk system, produced by the same company that makes applicant tracking systems, may prove to be a harbinger of the future for large organizations and corporations that are inundated with thousands of job seekers each year.

For human resource specialists, it is a tremendous savings of time and human effort, as well as paper, which adds up to a lot of energy and natural resources.

For more information on The Restrac Kiosk System, contact MicroTrac Systems, Inc., 1 Dedham Place, Dedham, MA 02026; Telephone (617) 320-5600; Fax (617) 320-5630.

HONESTLY, CAN YOU BE TRUSTED?

If you're going after a job in which you handle money or are in a position to pilfer goods, you may meet up with a computerized Pinkerton interview.

A number of large to midsize corporations employ one of the leading security firms, Pinkerton Security and Investigation Services, to screen and process job applicants, particularly when integrity is paramount.

Pinkerton offers to corporate America computerized interviewing and screening services that are designed to keep a company from taking on a bad hire, especially one who will pocket money or goods.

Beyond the honesty factor, a number of Pinkerton's clients say they use these evaluations because they result in significant reductions in turnover and workers' compensation.

At the heart of its extensive applicant screening process is Pinkerton's IntelliView program. IntelliView is a telephone-administered, computerized, structured interview you do using a Touch-Tone phone. The interview is in three parts:

1. A preliminary interview conducted with a computer. About 100 questions are asked in less than 10 minutes. The questions probe your past work history and attitudes that may affect your productivity.
2. An "interview folder" provides the interviewer with an organized method of documenting the telephone interview answers. It contains space to note your biographical information, work history, and reference evaluation. It also lists specific follow-up questions—based on answers you gave during the computer interview—to ask during the face-to-face interview.
3. A follow-up, face-to-face interview that focuses on your "key interview responses" to the computer interview.

Pinkerton says more than 1 million applicants each year use some form of pre-employment evaluation.

Company officials report more than 60 percent of applicants successfully pass through Pinkerton's extensive and intensive interview process.

Want more information? Contact Pinkerton's Information Center, 6100 Fairview Road, Suite 900, Charlotte, NC 28210; Telephone (800) 232-PINK; Fax (704) 554-1806.

EMPLOYMENT TESTS YOU MAY FACE

Because testing—as a part of screening—can knock you out of the box no matter how well you do in all other areas of the job search, you should know a few things about the tests you may be asked to take.

These aren't substance abuse tests. We're talking about the kind of quizzing you're likely to encounter when you interact with a computer.

Most thoughtful people agree that tests can never be free from bias. In a classic example, a whole class of Hawaiian kids flunked an intelligence test because, when asked to draw a house, not one drew a chimney. The explanation is simple: In their climate, none had ever seen a chimney.

Employment testing is with us to stay, and here are a few of the most prevalent types.

Success Rates of New Computerized Tests May Be Less Than Sterling

Testing has developed into big business in the United States. Nobody knows exactly how big, but estimates put it in the billions of dollars annually when all kinds of tests are included. The tests have a major influence on the Great American Sorting: they influence who gets hired, who gets promoted on the job, and who gets into which institution of higher education.

The value of testing—and now, computerized testing—is up for debate. Test makers insist their products are unbiased, relevant, and sound. But minorities, women, and others challenge the validity and fairness of the testing industry's products.

Fairtest, a Massachusetts advocacy organization, verbally cold-cocks the testing industry every chance it gets. Among its charges against computerized tests are:

1. Computerized tests may penalize mind changers because they can't underline the tests, rethink and scratch out choices, or work out math problems, all common strategies on paper-and-pencil tests. (Tip: Take a pad of scratch paper and pencils with you to employment tests.)

2. Computerized tests don't allow test takers to easily check previous items and the pattern of their responses, two other practices commonly used. Scrolling through multiple screens does not allow side-by-side comparisons.

3. Computerized tests may actually worsen bias. Computer anxiety is to blame for many low scores. Poor people and minorities are less likely to have computers at home.

Fairtest says automating tests does nothing to ease long-standing problems and may actually compound them.

Test makers say that criticism is nonsense.

You be the judge.

Integrity Tests

Employers want to find out whether you're light-fingered. Employee pilferage—not to mention embezzlement—costs businesses billions of dollars yearly.

Balanced against that understandable concern regarding your tendencies toward honesty are your right to privacy and the validity of the testing.

The integrity exams usually are not tricky. They go right to the point, asking frankly about theft or deception. What's amazing is how people will incriminate themselves on "impersonal" tests, as though it's okay to tell a computer anything.

Experts say high-risk persons rate themselves lower in honesty and in such related areas as use of illegal drugs than do others. The thieves among us tend to believe that most employees steal and make easy excuses for theft. ("Everybody does it.") They often think about stealing and make more admissions of petty theft than do others.

Some people who overrate their ability to outfox the test will, by being too goody-goody in their answers, reveal to test interpreters that they are purposely trying to affect the test results.

Here are some examples of true/false questions designed to unmask attempts at distorting results:

▶ I don't worry what others think of me.
▶ I've never stolen anything in my life.
▶ I've never stolen from an employer.
▶ I've never cheated on a test.
▶ I've never even considered cheating.
▶ I never have trouble sleeping at night.

If you try answering "true" to all of the above statements, you signal that you're faking it. Haven't you ever swiped a donut or a pencil? Haven't you at least considered cribbing on a test? Haven't you ever had a restless night?

Test publishers say no single answer is used as a basis of conclusions; instead, they look for a tendency shown in a series of answers throughout the test. Be aware of your tendencies in the types of responses you give.

Test critics say that the honesty tests are genuinely predictive only when big numbers of people are involved, and that user companies play the percentages. This means, to paraphrase scholars on the issue, that innocent people will be misclassified and wrongly denied jobs.

How can you protect yourself?

When you are asked to take an integrity test, ask how the results will be used. This inquiry opens the door for your follow-up statement:

"I'm sure you know there is some disagreement about the value of integrity tests, and that false positives sometimes occur. I think I read that somewhere. I'm very interested in this job. Will you let me know if anything negative should turn up on my test, so I can have the opportunity to speak to that concern? I don't expect anything, but I like to cover all the bases when there's something I really want. That's fair, isn't it?"

Job Skills Tests

"Can you do the job?" is the question behind job skills testing. The test may require hands-on performance or may involve a computerized exam.

Try to determine what most employers use as a job skills test, and anticipate how you can brush up for it. You can't study for the tests an employer will give; they're not like examinations of knowledge. But by being aware of what may be asked, you probably can better handle the pressure of being tested.

Personality Tests

You're good, but are you normal? That's what employers want to know when they require you to take a psychological test as part of your screening process.

Questions on personality tests are designed to pin down vocational interest traits—and to make sure you won't disturb the peace in the work environment even if you can do the job.

After you complete the personality test, the company ends up with a psychological profile of you which, accurate or not, can be used in decisions to hire, promote, or eventually fire you.

Computers are used to measure your raw scores against a "normative" group—people who have taken the test previously. If a group of successful engineers, for instance, tended to answer the test questions in a certain way, and you, as an engineer, answer those questions in the same way, you will be presumed to have the personality of a successful engineer.

The predictive validity of these tests depends on those for whom the tests were standardized. With our culture undergoing rapid change—by the year 2000, nearly 30 percent of the U.S.

population will be members of minorities—it's a challenge for test makers to stay current.

"There is a great deal of old-fashionedness built into these tests . . . cultural lag," according to William H. Whyte, author of *The Organization Man*, one of the blockbuster management books of the 1950s.

"They don't dare change the doggone things because then they can't say, 'We have tested this against 50,000 supervisory personnel.' The minute they change one question, they no longer can make that claim."

Whyte has interpreted this to mean that "unconsciously, the framers of the tests have enshrined the attitudes of some years ago."

Some people subscribe to the be-yourself school of testing. They say it's unwise to attempt to beat the personality tests by telling employers what you think they want to hear.

We're not so sure. An equally valid approach is to write a clear, concise personality statement in advance of job hunting. Declare who you think you are. Include your characteristics. List your strengths as they apply to the job you hope to land. Write as though you were describing a character in a film script.

Other job applicants are more cynical. They approach personality tests by forming a clear mental picture of a very successful friend in a similar career field. Then they concentrate on what they think their friend's attitudes would be toward the questions. This technique works for some people.

When it's personality test time, try to make your answers consistent for the character you have described, or to the mental image of a successful friend. It's wise to stay in character—but tilt toward conservatism.

If, for instance, you see such questions as "Which do you read first, (a) the financial pages or (b) the sports section?," or "Would you prefer to spend an afternoon (a) chopping wood or (b) digging ditches?" try to answer in a manner best fitting your character.

Here's one more tip to ace psychological tests: Avoid absolutes in answering most questions. The words "always" or "never" can be a trap. For example, "I've never taken more than my fair share of anything" should be marked false or you may be seen as too good to be true.

Bedknobs, Broomsticks, and Job-Seeking Wizardry

A Collage of High-Tech Tools for Choosing a Career, Landing a Job, and Moving Up

We have looked at ways to electronically make our qualifications visible to employers (Chapters 2 and 3). We have explored electronic pathways into the advertised (Chapter 4) and hidden (Chapter 5) job markets. And we have introduced the computer as interviewer and test giver (Chapter 6).

In this chapter, we review a medley of other electronic services for today's job market, developments that are excitingly new to most of us. The chapter ends with a preview of emerging technologies that will take our job searches further than ever before.

Think about the electronic revolution this way: Do you prefer that technology befriend or bedevil you?

Radical change is sweeping the job market—beyond even the dramatic developments we've explored in the preceding chapters.

Here are more changes. Some are measured in baby steps. Others have blockbuster potential. Even if you are not actively seeking a new job as you read, take this chance to get the high-tech lowdown on new ways to make the job market work for you. In a few words, make technology your new best friend. Finally, anticipate, with us, the beckoning job search frontier so that you can take good care of your future.

PASS THE TELEPHONE

We don't have to remind you that the telephone is one of the principal and most important tools in your job search. However, you may want information about some new and inexpensive resources via Uncle Alexander's little invention—resources that can make your life more interesting and possibly a lot easier as you embark on the hunt for your next job.

Career America Connection

How it benefits you: For the cost of a telephone call, usually less than $2 or $3 in long-distance charges, you can find out about all the open federal jobs for which you qualify. This is a real red-tape cutter and an admirable example of your tax dollars at work.

Many people still don't know about this first-rate federal government service. Career America Connection is a telephone system (you pay for long-distance calls) but it can be a real time saver, and time is money. The average call is about six minutes in length, at a typical cost of 25 cents or less per minute.

The U.S. Office of Personnel Management developed this system. Anyone interested in available federal jobs can call any day of the week, 24 hours a day, on either a rotary or Touch-Tone telephone. Make sure you have a pad of paper and a pencil or pen handy because lots of information is packed into a short amount of time.

After you're connected, you'll be asked to choose from a menu of options. Touch-Tone telephone users punch buttons on the dialing pad; rotary callers use voice commands the system will recognize. This means you just touch or talk your way to the information you want.

Career America Connection has two job information services: Career America College Hotline and the General Jobline.

The College Hotline contains information on entry-level jobs for college graduates nationwide. (This same information is available free at college career centers, job fairs, and public job service offices.)

College Hotline callers choose from such occupational categories as accounting, administrative, business and finance, engineering, law enforcement, medical and health careers, and science.

Although this service is aimed primarily at recent graduates, more seasoned job seekers who are considering entry-level or junior-level government positions can benefit by using the College Hotline.

The General Jobline adds to the College Hotline information, discussing jobs across the country at all levels.

"Job openings" are announcements of actual positions to be filled, but often the government lists "job opportunities" for anticipated openings within the near future at specific agencies. These opportunities announcements are usually a good indication that job openings will soon exist.

An example of this outcome occurred in 1981, when President Reagan threatened to fire striking FAA air traffic controllers. The "opportunities" announcement heralding the possibility of openings in the air traffic control field went out. A few days later, Reagan did what he promised and the "job opportunities" announcement was switched to a "job openings" announcement. The "job openings" announcement was posted for job vacancies that actually existed. The anticipation had become reality.

"Job opportunities" should be studied and considered as a good indication of what's in the wings. It's your cue to prepare and apply.

In addition to job openings and opportunities, callers can choose messages about federal salaries and benefits, how federal jobs are filled, special employment programs for veterans and people with disabilities, and student and intern programs. The information is fresh because it's updated daily.

Another plus for Career America Connection is that you're invited to leave voice-mail messages with your contact information, to receive application materials. These messages are processed the next business day so you'll probably get the information within a week.

Call Career America Connection at (912) 757-3000.

Career America Connection covers the range of jobs available throughout the federal government at any given time. Some departments and agencies of the government operate their own hotlines to maintain a tighter rein on their individual recruiting efforts. An example of a single agency hotline is the one operated by the Library of Congress in Washington.

The telephone number for the Library of Congress electronic job line is (202) 707-4315.

A DATABASE DESCRIBING FEDERAL JOBS

Considering the thousands of jobs and classifications within the federal government, you definitely need a road map to find where you're trying to go. What kinds of jobs are there today? In what department or agency? What are the requirements? The pay? The geographic location? Must you take a test?

For answers to questions like these, here is a program to help you cut through the bureaucratic maze of the federal government.

FOCIS

How it benefits you: Here's an easy way to get the scoop on federal job descriptions.

The Federal Occupational and Career Information System (FOCIS), a database, gives you a better handle on various occupations within the federal government.

You can look through library reference books, or you can go to most public employment service offices, college career centers, or your library, and ask to use the computer-driven FOCIS, Version 4. Or you can purchase the diskette yourself.

Prepared by the Office of Personnel Management, FOCIS describes more than 360 federal white-collar occupations likely to have the largest number of openings. Remember, these aren't actual openings; they are job descriptions in agencies where openings are likely to be frequent.

For each occupation, FOCIS gives a description of the work, minimum qualifications, grade levels, salaries, and addresses to contact.

Campus career center staffs across the nation are using electronics to put graduates together with employers. This program comes on a disk for use on a IBM-PC and compatible personal computers. Call the National Technical Information Service at (703) 487-4650.

Job Hotlines USA

How would you like to have more than 1,000 hard-to-find telephone numbers offering prerecorded lists of available jobs at companies and government agencies? For less that $30, including shipping, you can buy a copy of *Job Hotlines USA, The National Telephone Directory of Employer Joblines* from Career Communications Inc., 298 Main Street, P.O. Box 169, Harleysville, PA 19438; Telephone (215) 256-3130. Your library may have a copy.

Most joblines are not toll-free 800 numbers, but they are typically available 24 hours a day and you can save money by calling during off-peak hours and weekends. Have paper and pencil ready when you call.

CRAMMING FOR MORE THAN JUST FINAL EXAMS

If you're a recent college graduate, you don't have to be told that it's tough sledding on a crowded hill for that first job—particularly if you were a liberal arts major. Here's what a couple of leading universities are doing to help their graduates get jobs.

Ball State University

How it benefits you: As a Ball State graduate, you are on tap in your school's online database when employers call. Think of it as a graduation gift. If you're a job-seeking alum, consider it to be one more good reason you attended that school. If you're not a Ball State graduate, check with your alma mater and ask whether similar programs are available to you.

Within 48 hours of employers' inquiries to the Candidate Referral Service, offered by Ball State University in Muncie, Indiana, they're sent a list of graduating seniors or job-seeking alumni. The list is designed to keep them coming back for more.

The program has personal data forms, or, for lack of a better description, mini-resumes, on more than 3,000 individuals available to requesting employers.

Information fitting the job requisition is selected from the school's database and sent for the employer's consideration. Although many of the companies taking advantage of the service have been regional companies located in the Midwest, referral requests have come from as far away as the West Coast. One such request came from a California school district that was searching for an experienced school superintendent. Some employers say they like this type of service because it supplements their on-campus recruiting efforts.

University of Virginia

How it benefits you: As a University of Virginia graduate, your university is compensating for the falloff of recruiters from big companies who come to campus to recruit. It is moving your qualifications into the marketplace. If you're not a University of Virginia graduate, check with your school's career center to see what special programs are operating to help you.

The University of Virginia Office of Career Planning and Placement releases, on one 3.5-inch IBM/compatible disk, more than 1,250 student resumes for perusal by companies that no longer can afford or choose not to send recruiters to the campus.

The center mails the disk free to any business requesting it.

JOB DESCRIPTIONS HELP SHOW YOU HAVE WHAT THEY WANT

Any time you apply for a job, you're ahead of the pack when you know exactly the requirements of the position. This knowledge enables you to show how your qualifications are a good fit. If you can get a copy of the real job description from the advertising employer's human resource department, so much the better. Often, the real thing won't be available, so the next best thing is to visualize the duties and skills involved in the job.

On a sheet of paper, use the left side to write down what you think the job requires. On the right side, write down how you stack up. This comparison is immeasurably helpful in responding to a recruitment ad and for polishing your performance during the job interview. As an old saying goes, "You'll be loaded for bear."

Job Scribe

How it benefits you: Looking at job descriptions helps you sell yourself because it shows you know the tasks, lingo, and nature of the work.

This personal software for PCs enables you, the job seeker, to review accurate job descriptions. Job Scribe, Version 2.0 includes some 3,000 job descriptions. The program reportedly was developed using authentic job descriptions at all levels in actual organizations.

By using Job Scribe's data, you aren't trying to put one over on employers. You're not trying to come up with a phony resume with a rote listing of skills and experience that merely tells the employer what the employer wants to hear. You are, however, getting clues to appropriate language and terms to interpret your educational qualifications or work history.

Job Scribe, a reference tool rather than a home-use database, may be found at the reference desk of a large library, at school district offices, at city and county government complexes, and at college career centers.

JOB DESCRIPTIONS HELP SHOW YOU CAN DO WHAT THEY WANT

A refinement to the concept of using job descriptions to show you're a good match for the job has occurred since the passage of the Americans with Disabilities Act, now commonly known as ADA.

The passage of the ADA has swung open a big employment door long closed to many persons with disabilities. If you fit into this category, the next few paragraphs will be of substantial interest.

For the first time in history, job opportunities are available to the 70 percent of individuals with disabilities who are jobless—and don't want to be. Interviewers can no longer ask whether you have a disability, only whether you are able to perform the *essential functions of the position with or without reasonable accommodation.*

Despite ADA protection, the job world remains a jungle for the unwary who may—to their detriment—*inappropriately* blurt out a disability at the employment interview, or even on their resumes. Guard against that error by becoming informed on wise ways to use your new rights.

In this connection, here's an extra tip beyond reading job descriptions with an ADA twist. Buy or consult an outstanding book, *Job Strategies for People with Disabilities,* by Melanie Astaire Witt (Peterson's Guides, 1992). It is the first published effort to combine state-of-the-art career decision-making and employment-search techniques with the special interests of persons with disabilities. Quite simply, we think it's the single best career guide ever written for this readership.

The ADA will completely change the way American employers staff—exactly how, remains to be seen. Experts disagree about whether there will be an explosion of litigation.

Job descriptions are becoming more important: every word is being weighed against the ADA requirements. The ADA provides incentives for employers to plan ahead by creating written job descriptions before advertising or interviewing for positions.

A number of compliance tools are available to employers to help them cope with this rather complex law. As a job seeker, you will want to be aware of the lengths to which employers may go to ensure that all Americans—with or without disabilities—who want to work get an equal shot.

The following example of "ADA-safe" software is written to benefit employers who don't want to run afoul of the law. To discover the essential functions of a position—to help you know whether you can do the job with a reasonable accommodation—it's useful to step into the employer's shoes.

Where can you, the job seeker with a disability, screen the software? A straightforward call to the human resource department of a large company may get you an invitation. Ask whether the company has a diversity manager.

Here's another idea: Try a nearby "independent living center," which can be referred to you by the National Council on Independent Living, Troy Atrium, 4th Street and Broadway, Troy, NY 12180; Telephone (518) 274-1979 or (518) 274-0701. Names of centers vary. An example: The Access Center of San Diego, Inc.

If your local independent living center does not have an ADA-job-description database, its staff, being familiar with community resources for people with disabilities, may be able to suggest where else you might try.

DescriptionsWrite Now!

How it benefits you: If you have a disability, this job description program with ADA content can be used to determine whether you can do the work and how to position yourself in talking to employers.

This PC-based software program custom-writes complete job descriptions for the employer, in addition to facilitating every phase of employment to help comply with the ADA.

This program is for managers and employers who have little experience in writing job descriptions.

DescriptionsWrite Now! is available from KnowledgePoint, 1311 Clegg Street, Petaluma, CA 94954; Telephone (800) 727-1133. The program sells for less than $149.

In addition to the two above examples, a number of the applicant tracking systems we discussed in Chapter 3 offer tools within their programming to assist the employer in ADA compliance.

ADA protects individuals with physical or mental impairments, including those people who wish to return to work after such catastrophic events as a heart attack or cancer treatment.

By official count, nearly one in five adults in this country has a disability. Maybe you're that one. If not, you probably know someone who is eligible to be protected by ADA. It's useful to know that employers, often through electronic assistance, are making an effort to meet the federal mandate to level the playing field.

SOFTWARE JOB SEARCH TOOLS

Computers were designed to ease the routine stress in our lives, allowing us to concentrate on more productive efforts.

Record keeping in a job search can be a killer, but it's one of those VIDs—Very Important Details. Now you can handle much, if not all, of it with computer software.

Career Navigator

How it benefits you: This program and its extensive job search handbook gives experienced job seekers special help in landing the right job in a competitive marketplace.

Nationally recognized Drake Beam Morin, Inc., consultants in the human resource management field to corporate America, offers Career Navigator. This is a four-disk, IBM-compatible computer software program designed for entry-level to middle-level professionals.

Career Navigator includes an extensive job-search handbook, as well as many job-search letters that can be electronically created and stored within the system. It offers a series of tests, with scores and feedback assessing your communication style.

The program is available from Drake Beam Morin, Inc., 100 Park Avenue, New York, NY 10017; Telephone (212) 692-7700 or (800) 345-JOBS.

Electronic Job Hunter

How it benefits you: Here's a software program that automatically creates resumes and connects its users with an on-line employment network.

Job seekers who enroll in the On-Line Employment Network, a resume database, are called members. The Electronic Job Hunter package, for use on a PC, allows members to modem a detailed work history profile and resume to the service.

The package provides the communication software needed to link members directly to the network, as well as the software to create the profile form of 125 items and the resume.

Members can have themselves listed in one or more of five database categories: (1) intern/student, (2) graduate, (3) individual for hire, (4) consultant, and (5) contractor/temporary.

To be a member in the On-Line Employment Network, you buy a copy of the Electronic Job Hunter at a cost of less than $40. The software purchase includes a one-year membership in the network.

Employers—including educational, medical and governmental institutions, as well as recruiting firms and temporary services firms—pay a fee for unlimited network usage.

Individuals and employers communicate directly within the network's e-mail system, making this what is believed to be the first fully interactive system of its kind. How is confidentiality protected? Both job seekers and employers receive passwords and identification numbers. The interested party leaves a name and contact information in the e-mail box of the other.

Currently centered in the Southwest, the company says it plans wide expansion. For information on Electronic Job Hunter and On-Line Personnel Services, contact On-Line Personnel Services at P.O. Box 26852, Phoenix, AZ 85068; Telephone (602) 404-4388; Fax (602) 404-2931.

JobHunter

How it benefits you: This software allows your computer to be your secretary on an active job hunt.

Not to be confused with the above-described Electronic Job Hunter offered by On-Line Personnel Services, JobHunter is a software tool for organizing your job search.

For every person you contact, JobHunter, which will run on any IBM-compatible PC, creates a computer record by name, title, company, address, telephone, and fax numbers. The program reportedly provides frameworks for keyboarding cover letters, thank-you notes, confirmations, and so forth. It automatically addresses these communications to prospective employers you specify.

This $40 package can be ordered from Resumate (you read about this company's applicant tracking system in Chapter 3) by calling the company at (800) 530-9310, or by writing to it at P.O. Box 7438, Ann Arbor, MI 48107.

Sharkware

How it benefits you: This career management program brings new meaning to "It's whom you know that counts." Sharkware is the only total contact and activity management system for PCs. With this product, it's easy to stay in touch with your network of contacts that means so much to your lifetime success.

One of the newest software programs on the market includes advice and techniques from Harvey Mackay, top-ranked motivational speaker and author of *Swim with the Sharks Without Being Eaten Alive* and *Sharkproof.*

Sharkware, which requires a 386 (or higher) IBM-compatible PC, Windows 3.1, and a VGA color monitor (equipment many people have today), manages information important to your immediate job search as well as to your long-term career success.

It stars the Mackay 66, a 66-question profile on the care and feeding of contacts, a profile recognized as one of the author's most effective methodologies.

The easy-to-use computerized version of the Mackay 66 covers seven categories of information for each contact: (1) education, (2) family, (3) business background, (4) special interests, (5) lifestyle, (6) the user's relationship with the contact, and (7) traditional address book entries.

Additionally, Sharkware has features such as unlimited addresses and space for comments. It comes with a fully integrated appointment calendar, a "to-do" list space, and a telephone call manager.

Sharkware retails for less than $130. Find it in software stores, or order it through CogniTech Corporation, P.O. Box 500129, Atlanta, GA 31150; Telephone (404) 518-4577.

The Computer-Powered Job Search System

How it benefits you: As an entry-level job seeker, you get ace advice from one of the heavyweight outplacement consulting firms.

This software job search package by Drake Beam Morin, Inc., a leading outplacement consulting firm, offers advice and information to the novice.

Drake Beam Morin markets The Computer-Powered Job Search System through its DBM Publishing division. The comprehensive program, endorsed by the College Placement Council, operates on IBM-compatible PCs.

The package takes you through suggestions to identify prospects, select targets, develop approaches, prepare for interviews, and negotiate the job offer. The software, which comes on four disks, includes a 200-page manual with lots of true–false quizzes, worksheets, and short case studies.

For more information, write to Drake Beam Morin, 100 Park Avenue, New York, NY 10017; Telephone (800) 345-JOBS or (212) 692-7700.

WHEN THE COMPUTER IS YOUR COUNSELOR

Are you considering heading off in a new direction in your life, either because you want to or because you have to?

If so, you can get help recycling yourself with one of the new software packages designed to help you make career decisions. You'll want help with personal assessment in such areas as general interests, academic interests, work-related interests, general abilities, aptitudes, values, work environment preferences, education level, and choice of working with people, data, or things.

Remember, view these packages as the first step in your new direction, not the final decision. You'll need to supplement them with lots of first-hand research. Here are tools that can help.

Career Design

How it benefits you: This product is a bargain for career changers. It is the software version of the high-end career counseling method developed by the late John Crystal and his surviving partner, Nella Barkley. The seminar format lasts a week and costs several thousand dollars.

In development for ten years, Career Design is aimed at anyone who is considering a career change. The program is divided into more than 50 modules. Through a series of questions, they lead the career changer to such key realizations as: "Who am I?" "What do I really want?" "How do I get what I really want?"

Through interaction with the computer, you discover your interests and skills, how to set goals, how to negotiate, and how to cope with many other challenges you must master to change careers.

Career Design is attractive not only for its simplicity, comprehensiveness, and excellent value, but also for its in-depth expertise. You won't need an extra book to use it.

At least one software reviewer wrote that it takes a minimum of 40 hours to work through the Career Design's program. What apparently was overlooked by that writer is that it takes months to reflect on the crucial issues of who you are, who you want to be, where you want to go, and to which company or industry you will sell your life.

Career Design works on any IBM-compatible PC and is available for under $100 from Career Design Software, P.O. Box 95624, Atlanta, GA 30347; Telephone (800) 346-8007.

Peterson's Career Planning Service

How it benefits you: Specific occupations are suggested for your aptitudes, interests, temperament, and values. Information is given on how to research occupations.

This reference desk tool may be available at libraries, college career centers, and public employment service offices.

It contains information on occupations, related jobs, training and education requirements, and occupational profiles. The computer program is designed to assist you in making good career decisions.

You complete a wide variety of personal assessment exercises and relate the results to occupational options. The program corresponds in part to the Peterson's College Database. It's like having your own career counselor, but at less cost.

Available for IBM in 5.25-inch and 3.5-inch formats, Peterson's Career Options sells for under $300. For more information, contact Peterson's, P.O. Box 2123, Princeton, NJ 08543.

Shareware: "Looking for Work"

How it benefits you: The shareware concept lets you try a software program on the cheap, usually for a few dollars. If it works for you, you're honor-bound to pay the full price of the program. It's a bargain.

Shareware is like a self-published book—it's software that has been written by an electronic author who hasn't hit prime time as yet. More often than not, the quality of shareware is top-notch. It usually costs less than $4 or $5 to try.

It's called "shareware" because the author is "sharing" his or her program with you. The publisher is trusting you, hoping that if you can use it, you'll pay what the software is really worth. The requested full payment for shareware usually runs between $5 and $100.

Virtually any vendor offering shareware will have at least one or two job search software programs. They are like new television sets—all of them will work, but you'll like the picture on some better than on others.

One we like very much, which comes highly recommended from outplacement firms that have used it extensively, is: Looking for Work: An Interactive Guide to Marketing Yourself.

Looking for Work is an interactive guide designed for professionals and managers who seek to change jobs or who have been laid-off or fired. Many have never been through a job search and need substantial help on even the most basic tasks and activities. Others will gain from a systematic approach.

The instructional software takes you step-by-step through eight units of instruction, augmented by dozens of worksheets to guide your job search.

The theme is that a job search is a marketing campaign and requires planning, analysis, targeted markets, and commitment to a schedule of tasks and activities. The program features a multi-track; that is, it directs you to the track best able to help you based on your age, income, current employment status, motivating factors, willingness to relocate, and level in the organization. This is a great feature because it goes straight to your bottom line.

When you complete the program, you will have a list of potential employers, a core resume, and marketing letters, and you will be prepared for interviews.

Specifically, the Looking for Work program will:

1. Help you develop a personalized plan, including a timetable and specific activities.
2. Help analyze your financial resources.
3. Give guidelines on preparing lists of target companies and other sources.
4. Provide forms, information, and guidance in preparing a detailed employment history.
5. Teach you how to prepare industry-specific resumes and marketing letters.
6. Structure week-by-week lists of tasks and activities, and identify milestones you can use to gauge your progress.
7. Identify online job listing and resume banks that may be appropriate for your experience and show why traditional resumes are unlikely to be effective.

8. Prepare you for what to expect in job interviews, including standard questions that may come your way.

You can obtain an examination copy of Looking for Work for less than $5. If you think it helps you, the full licensing fee for the new edition is $29. (Licensing for institutional use is priced professionally; query the publisher. A $49 retail edition also is offered to recent college graduates.)

Looking for Work is written and published by InterDigital, Inc., 25 Water Street, Lebanon, NJ 08833; Telephone (908) 832-2463. It works on any IBM-compatible PC.

Other employment software is available, too. Because of the nature of shareware publishing, we may never know how many employment-related programs are available at any one time, but the numbers are large. Software Labs (100 Corporate Point, Suite 195, Culver City, CA 90231; Telephone (800) 569-7900), for example, is a leading shareware vendor that lists a number of job search software programs. At less than $5 per program, you can order them all and discard what you don't want to use. If you do find one of use—and feel strongly about it—do be a straight shooter and send the author the requested contribution.

Shareware software is like a book; it cannot be read by two different persons at the same time. The software can be used by any number of people as long as it stays available for use at one location at a time.

Your new job may be mere keystrokes away.

TOOLS FOR HELP IN WRITING RESUMES

Using software to produce your resume has two big advantages over old-style typewriting and printing:

1. Greater flexibility to tailor the document to varying objectives.
2. Low-cost production of quality resumes.

You don't really need a computer program to punch out quality resumes, but it may be the path of least resistance for a neophyte resume writer.

A visit to your computer software store will show a wide variety of choice. Here are a few examples to illustrate the genre.

Instant Resume System

How it benefits you: The software makes writing your resume easier.

Martin John Yates is one of America's best known authorities on resumes. This program was adapted from his best-selling *Resumes That Knock 'Em Dead*. The Instant Resume System is an IBM-compatible program, sells for less than $60, and is easy to operate.

The program is available from LightningWord Corporation, 6558 Hampton Drive, San Jose, CA 95120; Telephone (800) 462-2571.

Look at other excellent all-around resume software programs, too, such as Yana Parker's ReadyToGo Resumes, Spinnaker's PFS: Resume & Job Search Pro, and Individual Software's ResumeMaker. All resume-writing programs are low-level word processors formatted with templates of various types of resumes.

Quick & Easy 171

How it benefits you: This software helps you prepare a high-quality federal job application.

At a time when it costs as much as $12.50 a page or more for typing of resumes and job application forms, this IBM-compatible program can save you money. It allows you to quickly and easily complete and print the federal Form SF-171. This latest, excellent version of the software supports some 50 popular printers and can print an exact facsimile of Form SF-171 and your data on standard blank paper.

It is available for under $50 from DataTech Software, 6360 Flank Drive, Harrisburg, PA 17112; Telephone (717) 652-4344.

PowerWords

How it benefits you: Want to seem "in the know" and eminently eligible for hire? Here's a niche program that helps you use buzz words in federal job applications.

This program is designed as a companion software package for Quick & Easy 171 (see above). It checks your completed Form SF-171 and makes suggestions about words that can be changed to produce a more powerful presentation of your experiences and skills. You get a discount when it's ordered along with Quick & Easy 171. PowerWords, under $30, is available from DataTech Software, 6360 Flank Drive, Harrisburg, PA 17112; Telephone (717) 652-4344.

SOON: USE E-MAIL TO CONTACT EMPLOYERS

E-mail (or *email*, according to *The New Hacker's Dictionary*) is flashing fast: It is sent and received within seconds—or minutes, at most. All you need is access to an online information service, an e-mail program, and the e-mail address of the person with whom you wish to communicate.

Rising career stars, particularly those with a technical bent, are beginning to send unsolicited resumes and cover letters by e-mail to selected employers. E-mail can be limited to a single recipient or it can reach out and touch hundreds of employers.

At this writing, there are two sticking points with using e-mail for targeted job search.

The first is that e-mail is not very secure. Once you send an e-mail message into the ether, you have no control over its privacy. Online correspondence easily can be saved, called up at a later date, and sent out to a large number of people. Unless you are unemployed, or unless you don't care whether your employer finds out you're on the march, choose other methods of transmitting your confidential resume.

The second problem with e-mail in the job search is that finding e-mail addresses can be difficult. E-mail addresses are beginning to appear on business cards and in some business directories, but comprehensive online directory assistance isn't available yet, as it is for telephone numbers. You can, of course, call the target executive's office and ask for the e-mail address.

A thorough discussion of how to use e-mail, plus tips for good guessing at e-mail addresses, can be found in *The Internet Companion* by Tracy LaQuery with Jeanne C. Ryer (Addison-Wesley, 1993). This book will turn you from "outsider" to "insider" in the new electronic information frontier.

MEET THE ELECTRONIC CAREER CENTER

It was bound to happen: a one-stop computer resource for career decision making. This concept is broader than Career Design, Peterson's Career Planning Service, and the shareware products described earlier in this chapter.

Once out of school, career choosers and career risers needed someplace to turn for vocational planning assistance. Of life's decisions, zeroing in on the right career field is one of the most tortuous for many people.

Here's a brief look at a prototype career guidance service.

America Online's Career Center

How it benefits you: An experienced career counselor with an academic background guides this service, which makes available resources that are difficult to find in some locales.

Within the Career Center, available through America Online (see Chapter 4), three services are offered:

1. *Career Counseling*—an option available at no additional fee beyond the normal America Online charges. You make an appointment electronically and talk, via computer, to a career counselor.
2. *Career Focus 2000*—another option available at no additional fee beyond the normal America Online charges. This is a series of four "workbook" exercises you download (a computer sends the data to your computer) and print.
   Booklets 1 and 2 constitute an interest inventory—what you like to do. The interest inventory allows you to compare your strongest interests with occupations, to find possible matches. Booklet 3 is a guide to decision making, and booklet 4 covers career planning. Completing the booklets may take several weeks and requires library research.
3. *Career Analysis Service*—the deluxe version of the other two options. Designed for people who need heavy-duty guidance in identifying occupations, this option costs under $40.

You should never make firm career decisions based only on tests; they are merely tools, not a course in Fate 101. View this counseling help as a starting place from which you will follow up with additional research, both primary (talking with people in the field of your interest) and secondary (reading up on it).
   Contact Career Center through America Online, 8619 Westwood Center Drive, Vienna, VA 22182; Telephone (800) 827-6364.

Dr. Job

How it benefits you: Ask questions and get answers about career matters that puzzle you.

This is a GEnie online careers advice column where subscribers can ask questions. Topics covered range from corporate politics to career decisions. Dr. Job answers as many questions as possible. Some of the questions may be used for future Dr. Job online columns. Information is kept confidential upon request, and names are not used.

To access, contact GEnie, 401 North Washington Boulevard, Rockville, MD 20850; Telephone (800) 638-9636.

NEW TOOLS EMPLOYERS USE TO SCREEN AND TEST APPLICANTS

As a job seeker in an ocean of others who are looking for a safe harbor, you already know that most employers have tightened the screening and testing techniques for their hiring process. Some companies are using comprehensive electronic programs, such as those discussed in Chapter 6, to accept applications and screen job seekers. Other programs are narrower in function, and, in fact, may be computerized versions of paper-and-pencil tests or of hands-on skill testing.

The two examples of electronic screening and testing noted below are designed to be used by employers. As a job seeker, you should know what human resource specialists are looking for and checking on when they begin considering your resume and application. Forewarned is forearmed.

Employment Research Services

How it benefits you: Score well and you'll probably get an offer; score poorly and you should keep looking.

Employment Research Services of Atlanta, with offices in a number of cities across the nation, offers custom-designed screening programs for companies' computer systems.

Programs prepared by Employment Research Services closely probe an applicant's references, past performance, skill level, salary history, employee–employer relations, criminal history, driving record, and credit history.

The Interviewer

How it benefits you: If you score well, you become a prime candidate; if you don't, you're probably out of luck.

Global Publishing Corporation of Provo, Utah, produces this inexpensive job applicant screening computer software for employers. The Interviewer concentrates on such positions as secretary, office manager, receptionist, bookkeeper, and administrative assistant, but ranges to all entry-level-type jobs.

Testing of a job seeker's skills in such computer programs as Windows, WordPerfect, Microsoft Word, Lotus 1-2-3, Quattro Pro, and Excel is available, as well as tests on subjects like math, grammar, typing, spelling, and so on.

Once the job seeker has completed the process on The Interviewer, the data are stored in the employer's database and can be accessed easily for review.

ENTREPRENEURSHIP: HIRING YOURSELF

Are you the sort of person who wants to break away from the world of wages and work for yourself? Perhaps you want to start your own small business. Perhaps you just want to pad the way for a more comfortable retirement by putting your hours away from your regular job into a part-time business that will earn extra cash.

Whatever your motive, you'll need all the information you can lay hands on, from software programs that write a business plan to a way to stay in touch with people who can help you nourish your fledgling business.

Among the resources you should check are those that find businesses to buy, locate people with special skills, or put you in touch with others who share your problems.

Business Resource Directory

How it benefits you: This is like an "electronic yellow pages" plus an electronic reference library plus an electronic personnel service—all rolled into one.

A searchable online database, Business Resource Directory is published and maintained by the National Small Businesses Network. It is available on GEnie's online information service. The Business Resource Directory is a good marketing tool for businesses, as well as individuals looking for work.

It's a way for individuals and businesses to locate other small businesses, home workers (people who want to work at home but not start their own business), job seekers, products, services, suppliers, and government offices that offer help to little-guy businesses.

The Business Resource Directory lists trade magazines, associations, government agencies, wholesalers, distributors, service bureaus, and software programs.

To subscribe, contact GEnie, 401 North Washington Boulevard, Rockville, MD 20850; Telephone (800) 638-9636.

Home Office/Small Business RoundTable

How it benefits you: This special-interest group service allows you to talk to others anywhere in the nation who may have problems similar to yours—and learn about their solutions. You're among friends here.

An online resource on GEnie, the Home Office/Small Business RoundTable is designed to meet the informational and networking needs of owners of micro- and home-based businesses or those who want to start a business.

The Home Office/Small Business RoundTable offers three categories of information about starting and operating a small or home-based business:

1. *The Bulletin Boards*—part of the GEnie basic online service. This is the main activity center where subscribers introduce themselves, write comments or ask questions about business, and "talk" to each other—with the help of their computer keyboards, of course. Most questions left in the Bulletin Boards are answered within 24 to 48 hours by either Home Office/Small Business RoundTable staff or members.

2. *Electronic Reference Libraries*—thousands of files, including how-to information and shareware (low-cost software) and freeware (free software) programs for businesses.

3. *Real Time Conference Rooms*—GEnie's version of computerized conferencing. Conferencing is a many-to-many medium, not a one-to-one form of communication. Everybody gets in on the act. Your messages are available for everyone in the conference to read and respond to, and you can react to the reactions. Conferencing is somewhat like a combination of a call-in radio talk show and a conference telephone call, only it takes place on the computer.

Contact GEnie, 401 North Washington Boulevard, Rockville, MD 20850; Telephone (800) 638-9636.

NATIONAL COMPUTER BULLETIN BOARD NETWORKS

Just when you thought you were getting a firm handle on electronic terms, someone asks if you've tried any "echoes" in your job search. Back to the dialog dictionary.

An "echo" is a network of electronic bulletin board services (BBS) that join hands to form an electronic mail system. Here's how it works.

You leave your message, or "mail," on a single BBS. The BBS sends (copies) your message to another BBS in the network. That BBS, in turn, sends your message—adding its own messages—to yet another BBS. And so on, until every BBS in the network, or echo, is sharing your message with its users. This is known as echoing, or relaying.

"Echoes" come in as many hundreds of flavors as the users who want to share special-interest conferences, such as the National Job Conference. But they all have a common goal: To provide an environment for the friendly exchange of messages with others all over the United States—and the world.

Some "echo" names you may hear are RelayNet, RIME, and FIDO. RIME is worldwide, including sites throughout the United States, Canada, Europe, Russia, South America, and the Far East. It includes more than 350 special-interest conferences and 975 computers exchanging information daily.

A little detective work will put you in touch with a member of one of these networks. If that "echo" isn't carrying a jobs conference, ask a system operator who runs a BBS on the network to start one.

Nearly every community in which you find a BBS will have someone who acts as a network "echo" site (often, a computer tied to an informational exchange network).

Access to an "echo" conference is frequently free. However, more and more BBS system operators are asking individuals to help defer the cost of their long-distance telephone bills.

Strict rules of courtesy apply to conference users; no wonder, with messages popping up in a matter of hours or days on hundreds of computer screens in Anytown, USA.

To illustrate the electronic power of a BBS, follow this country-crossing exchange. Kerry Goodwin in Dallas made online comments about this book. The next morning, our fax machine in southern California rang with a note from Donna Frappier, of Chicopee, Massachusetts. Frappier operates a free BBS that lists U.S. jobs available to candidates with a minimum of one year's work experience in the computer field. To reach Frappier's BBS, Career Systems Online, call: Modem (413) 592-9208 or Fax (413) 592-9255.

For jobs, support your local bulletin board and reach out to America.

INTERNET: NETWORK OF NETWORKS

Think back to the failed coup that sealed the fate of the Soviet Union in 1991. With Gorbachev, the media, and democracy held hostage,

Relcom (*Rel*iable *Com*munications), a small network in Moscow, became for a time the Soviet people's only source of news on the coup. How did the Relcom news get through to the outside world? Like bottled lightning; it crackled through on Internet, the network of networks.

Internet is an international network that includes virtually every major computer site in the world, and connects more than 8,000 networks spanning the globe. It is not an online service like those described in Chapter 4, but it is a resource of almost unimaginable wealth. In part, Internet is supported by the U.S. government.

For job seekers, Internet offers countless opportunities to make a connection with employment by posting resumes to relevant "newsgroups." These are forums for all kinds of interests and topics, from job hunting and real estate to aviation and fitness. By diligent searching, you'll find both formal job databases and informal job listings on Internet.

Futurists insist we're at the birth of a new era, and Internet literacy will be the basis for personal, business, and political advancement in the next century. As Alvin Toffler says in his 1990 book, *Power Shift*, "[Electronic] networks are the key infrastructure of the 21st century, as critical to business success . . . as the railroads were in Morse's era."

Today, Internet is used by businesspeople, journalists, librarians, educators, students, and hobbyists. It literally has become a window on the world.

Learning to use Internet can be compared to learning to drive. You have to make the effort to master the equipment and learn how to navigate the bumps on the electronic highways—or else content yourself with walking.

You can open the doors to Internet individually, with your computer and modem, or through companies where you work, schools where you teach or study, or libraries.

For specifics, read an inexpensive book mentioned on page 182, *The Internet Companion, A Beginner's Guide to Global Networking*.

A heftier tour guide to Internet's electronic corridors is *The Internet Navigator: A New User's Guide to Network Exploration* by Paul Gilster (John Wiley & Sons, 1993). This book shows individual computer users—including those who have never been attached to a network—the nitty gritty of gaining access to and moving through Internet. This book is an enormous help because there is no single Internet governing body, no single place to sign up and secure a password, and no single set of menus to guide new members.

Of the numerous ways to tap into Internet, the following access providers offer individual link-up, often with local area codes to save you money: WorldLink, Telephone (800) NET-2YOU; and THE WORLD, Telephone (617) 739-WRLD.

We'd tell you more, but we, too, are new to Internet and are not yet sufficiently familiar with its intricacies to become information brokers.

Academic Position Network

The Academic Position Network (APN) is an online academic position announcement service. It uses Internet, linking thousands of colleges and universities around the world.

Academic position announcements are transmitted to the APN office by e-mail or fax and placed on the network for immediate access worldwide.

Individuals seeking information about open academic jobs can access APN files through Internet/Gopher. Gopher, developed by the University of Minnesota, is a software system that is available, at no cost, for most PCs.

Learn more from the Academic Position Network, 245 East Sixth Street, Suite 815, St. Paul, MN 55101; Telephone (612) 225-1433.

TRACKING YOUR CAREER AFTER YOU'RE HIRED

Once you've settled on your job and are off on a new career adventure, don't think for a minute that the new employment rules and tools are out of your life.

The applicant tracking systems described in Chapter 3, in effect, are used to do employee tracking after the hire.

From your rising-star viewpoint, post-hire employee tracking systems have two things going for them: (1) job posting and (2) internal recruitment.

In job posting, job vacancies are up for everyone to see. In manual systems, a notice is simply posted on a company bulletin board. When an electronic tracking system is in place, you fire up your computer and search the job openings, applying for those you want and think you can get.

In internal recruitment, however, the job may or may not be posted. Your resume—with all its keywords intact—is in the company database, just waiting to be called up. A human resource specialist fires up the company computer and searches for a match.

With the new technology available, most companies using tracking systems will perform an internal search of current employees before going outside to fill a job.

When you upgrade your credentials with additional education, find out from your company's human resource department how you go about adding that information to your employee file.

Beyond job posting and internal recruitment possibilities, you'll be glad to know that, with the help of your new employer's human resource department, you can probably find in a flash the key information about your employment. Many employee tracking systems continue to enter facts into your records once you're on board.

Aside from the obvious information—your name, address, physical description, educational background, and work experience previous to your employment (in other words, your resume)—employee tracking systems keep tabs on virtually all employment-related matters. These include your job title, salary history, benefits, equal employment opportunity classification, division or department assignment, performance evaluations, work review dates, next scheduled performance evaluation, and next salary review.

The employee tracking system records the amount of vacation you've earned. It tallies overtime or comp time records, and notes your insurance expiration date and how many insurance premium payments have been made and by whom. The software records your income tax and social security data, plus any payroll withholding information.

Some programs have complete background information on your family, your dependents and their dates of birth, and emergency contacts—information necessary for all sorts of insurance and emergency purposes.

Many employee tracking systems keep records of all officially required safety and injury data. Companies that offer retirement programs maintain complete records with the magic of employee tracking systems.

ON THE HORIZON

If some of the technological whistles and buzzers we've described thus far have your mind spinning, brace yourself for the pathway into the next century. As we become increasingly aware of the role electronics plays in our work—the very foundation of our lives—we will want to pay more attention to the changing tools and the changing rules.

In our visions of tomorrow's workplace, the most startling new tool we see is digitized information dressed up in a wardrobe of new applications.

Trend followers know that information is going digital. Text, sound, and pictures all are being translated into those same zeros and ones that computers read. High-definition television (HDTV), ready to make its debut, is but one example of digital technology.

Bill Gates, the young and dazzling CEO of Microsoft, calls the technotrend "the new digital world order."

To back up a bit, our children may be more familiar with digital technology than some of us. They buy current forms of digital information in the disguise of CD music and laser video disks. These are the infant beginnings of tomorrow's version of the job search revolution.

Digitization doesn't just mean superior sound and video; it's a new dimension of random access to information. It wouldn't be much fun if you had to search a database from A to Z to find what you wanted, which might end up being located in V or Y. But when you can dive immediately into the target—the Vs or the Ys—the search is much easier, whether you are a job seeker or an employer. Smart searching is one of the attractive features of digitization.

If companies such as Sony and Phillips get to call the shots, it will be CD-ROM (Compact Disk-Read Only Memory) technology that leads the parade in bringing digital technology to center stage in the job search arena.

We know that a CD-ROM disk can put an encyclopedia in your pocket. (Among others, the 21-volume Grolier's Academic American Encyclopedia has been crammed into a 4³/₄-inch compact disk.) Now that the CD has come to computers, the video interview takes on new meaning.

Video interviews began in the 1970s and continued into the 1980s. An interviewer, usually off-camera, bounced questions to the job seeker (on-camera). After five or ten minutes, the interviewer called it a "wrap" and put the video cassette in a mailing case for shipment to prospective employers. In the beginning, executive recruiters perfected the video interview technique; later, entrepreneurs were franchised to do it for job seekers. Video interviewing never really caught on, partly because most employers didn't have a VCR handy to play the cassettes.

But now picture this: An employer sits in her office using a desktop computer to scroll through a group of applicants for a job opening she's trying to fill. She makes an initial selection of four candidates. Their full-text resumes read well.

"I wonder what they look and sound like in living color," she ponders. A command to a CD-ROM player, which is linked to her computer, pulls up the requested video interview lickety-split.

There, filling the computer screen, is candidate number one—answering questions, speaking, shifting in his chair, smiling, trying to look authoritative, trying to sell himself on screen.

"Well," the employer thinks to herself, "I'm underwhelmed with this one. On to the next . . . ." And so it goes until the "right" candidate is identified. "Let's fly this candidate out for a look-see," she says. Her company has saved a ton of money on personal interviews.

Less dramatic technology makes possible "motion-picture" representations of job seekers. Videophones—those long-promised telephones with picture screens that permit you to see the person with whom you're speaking—are finally with us after decades of false starts. They are still primitive, but you can buy them in office superstores for under $1,000. Once the technology becomes clearer, cheaper, and commonplace, many job interviews—particularly the first in a series of interviews—will take place on the videophone.

THE YEAR 2000—AND MAYBE BEFORE

Much of the future looks promising—and different. Here are some of the coming attractions.

1. *We rarely will travel to interviews. Electronic stand-ins will be sent in our place.*

Online services and applicant databases will grow, not only because employers find them to be cost-savers but because it is becoming easier to search and identify with scalpel-like precision.

An employer interviewed for this book was astounded to learn about the existence of applicant databases and online searching. He's been so busy tilling his vineyards he hasn't had time to become aware of the technology. After we told him how electronic search could, like a heat-seeking missile, zero in on qualified job seekers, he became excited. "Wow!," he said. "You mean there are services that do *that*? Give me some names of these services. This is a godsend."

As word gets around about the electronic job market, and as it becomes blazingly quick to transmit digitized information and images over telephone lines, it will be a relative breeze to keep yourself available and on display all the time, without your boss finding out you're looking.

Technology already exists to create an electronic superhighway—the kind that does for information what the interstate highway does for autos and trucks. It's called ATM, short for asynchronous transfer mode. We could call it "another technological marvel" because it's able to send digitized information at more than 45,000 times the speed available on typical telephone lines. It's tough for the mind to imagine speed faster than light, but ATM is a real whizzer. It can send the equivalent of 15,000 copies of *Moby Dick* in one minute.

ATM transmission of video, voice, and data is, at this writing, so fiendishly expensive that it will probably be a decade before the electronic superhighway begins to take shape. Even so, as modems become ever faster, growing numbers of employers will find out about the central-casting facilities available in the electronic universe and will hook in and hire up.

2. We will not let a good job get in the way of getting a better one. Even when employed, we'll look for brighter opportunities 24 hours a day, thanks to electronic magic.

No more sneaking around lining up job leads, hoping the boss doesn't find out we're on the market. We'll become our own opportunity managers around the clock, 365 days a year.

Tomorrow's digital technology, which we are breaking in today, will allow job seekers to create "personal documents" to take the place of paper resumes. Personal documents will combine text, sound, still pictures—and, yes, video.

This will be the ultimate video interview, combining the entire works. Personal documents will be passed from one computer to another over telephone lines—someday, over an electronic superhighway. The documents will be stored on a CD-like cassette or disk for delivery to a prospective employer.

The easier, faster, and cheaper the technology becomes, the more personal documents will be used—particularly for those whose graphic skills are critical, such as architects, journalists, advertising specialists, artists, and designers.

3. We will become three-dimensional job applicants rather than flat-paper cutouts.

Digitization will unchain us from geographical confinement. Looking for a job miles away has always been a challenge. Even when you do advance scouting by subscribing to newspapers in the targeted locale, and then network to line up job interviews and use your vacation days to do the interviews, your efforts usually aren't enough. Murphy's Law seems to have been invented for the long-distance job search: the people you most want to see are always out of town and will return "next week." Long-distance job hunts are possible, but they demand resourcefulness, savvy, tenaciousness, and luck.

When online recruitment advertising and personal documents become commonplace—and perhaps the norm for professional and managerial personnel—finding employment outside your immediate locale will be far less of a hassle. Even networking in a new locale will be facilitated when you can telephone a friend's friend in another city and say, "Hold on a sec; let me pop over my personal document. I'd appreciate it if you'd take a look and suggest whom I should be talking to in your city."

4. *Long-distance job hunting will become an easy stretch without leaving home.*

Another application of digital technology—one that is actually quite close—is the 500-channel-capacity television system, which is expected to be here circa the mid-1990s. Cable companies will be scrambling for ways to fill all that channel capacity created by digital compression.

Expect an explosion of the kinds of services described in this book, perhaps with entire channels being devoted to issues of career choice, job search, and career development.

In a related development, home entertainment centers gradually are becoming available to Americans who don't earn as much as rock music stars. Still pots-of-money expensive, prices for the electronic hubs are expected to fall as the decade rolls toward the new century.

Among the speculations, the futuristic home entertainment centers are envisioned as combining, in one piece of equipment, four major in-home communicating technologies:

1. Telephone.
2. Audio/video receiving (radio and television).
3. Audio/video recording (VCR).
4. Interactive informational computing (PC computer).

You could do a whale of a job search using your interactive television console as a tool. You would have access to any of those 500-plus channels of TV and informational online services, and could use the console for your personal, interactive communications.

5. *Cable television may become our primary employment center.* This development, if it happens, certainly is in the coming century. Visionaries see it as a logical extension of digital wizardry.

AND, FINALLY . . .

We enjoyed flapping our futuristic wings on these last few pages. One of the best jobs going is that of long-term forecaster because you'll be dead before the world knows whether you were right or wrong.

We are sure the job search revolution we've reported in this book—and in our companion guide, *Electronic Resume Revolution*—has begun and is picking up steam today. Gathering the information about what's happening has made believers of us. But our crystal ball is as hazy as anyone else's about the exact turn of events several decades from now. We've reported to you what we think will happen, based on the direction in which the job market is moving.

In any case, as new tools continue to appear, here are two rules to remember:

1. Technology is moving job search to the people, not people to the job search.
2. Ignore the job search revolution at your own risk. It's the change of the century. Start now to learn the new ropes—and gain The Big Edge.

Computer Terms Made Simple

analog Numerical values represented by physical variables such as voltage, current. Analog devices are characterized by dials and sliding mechanisms. See also *digital*.

application software Computer programming allowing the user to perform specific tasks such as word processing or accounting.

ASCII A universal code most desktop computers understand. Shorthand for American Standard Code for Information Interchange, and pronounced "askee." It's not easy reading.

audio Sounds for the human ear used by multimedia systems.

baud A measurement of speed at which information is transferred over a modem from one computer to another. Similar to BPS (bits per second), but not exactly the same. Computer buffs say the term "baud" is outdated and BPS is more accurate. But, right or wrong, you'll see the terms used interchangeably. The workhorse BPS speed today is 2400. Many people have 9600 BPS modems, or 14,400 BPS modems. The higher the number, the faster the information zips along telephone lines and the cheaper your telephone bill (if you're paying).

BBS Bulletin board system—a computer that has been connected to a telephone line through a modem. Computer users can then phone a specific BBS and swap information, computer files, programs, or fellowship. An electronic meeting place where users with common interests exchange information.

binary system A code that translates all letters and numbers into combinations of ones and zeroes. As a job seeker, you really don't care, but the term is so common you should know what it means.

bit The smallest unit of computer information—either a one or a zero.

BPS Bits per second. See *baud*.

byte The amount of space it takes to store a single character on a disk—usually a chunk of four to eight bits, representing a single number, letter, or other character. The word "dog" takes three bytes of information.

CD Compact disk—optically read disk. CDs can hold a ton of information. Machines read them.

CD-I Compact disc-interactive—a compact disk format that provides audio, digital data, still graphics, and limited motion video. For a presentation, it's the works!

CD-ROM Compact disk-read only memory—a way to permanently store mountains of data.

central processing unit Called the CPU, it's the brain of the computer.

character One letter, number, or figure.

chips Very small squares or rectangles holding electronic circuits. Chips hold from a few dozen to several million electronic components, such as transistors and resistors. The terms *chip, integrated circuit,* and *microelectronic* all mean the same thing.

clone A copy of an existing computer design.

compatible A term used to describe computers capable of operating the same software.

computer literacy A state of being fluent in computerese.

computer program A very specific, very explicit, set of instructions given to a computer to perform a task or tasks.

computerese A special language spoken by users, power users, hackers, and nerds. You can become old and gray before you become fluent in computerese. Words like "upload" and "digitize" are prime examples. Upload means to get the stuff up and out of your computer and into somebody else's computer. *Digitize* is described below.

DAT Digital audio tape—a consumer recording and playback medium for high-quality audio.

data Information.

database A structured collection of related information. A common example is a computerized file of resumes that a computer can call up on command.

desktop publishing The function of creating complex documents that integrate text, graphics, and different styles of type. Some job seekers who understand desktop graphics junk up their resumes trying to use all the available bells and whistles.

device A general term for a piece of equipment attached to the computer. See *peripheral device*.

digital The use of numbers. The word is derived from digit, or finger. Today, digital is synonymous with computer.

digitize   Convert information to binary codes—the ones and the zeros.

directory   A summary of the information contained in a computer or on a disk, as well as a map of how to locate that information; similar to a table of contents.

disk   A storage device within a computer, usually called the computer's "hard drive" or "hard disk," or a floppy disk that moves from computer to computer.

disk drive   Computer hardware; utilizes floppy disks, hard disks, or both.

disk operating system   Commonly known as DOS—a very basic software program allowing the computer to obey your commands as well as the commands of application software. MS-DOS and Windows are two well-known disk operating systems.

display   What you see on the computer screen (monitor).

document   A file such as a "text" produced by a word processing program.

dot matrix   A simple type of printer that utilizes pins to imprint tiny dots of ink onto paper. For resumes, if you use a dot matrix printer, make sure it's a 24-pin dot matrix to achieve near-letter quality.

dots per inch   Usually noted as DPI; refers to the quality of print or graphics, as measured by the density of individual dots of ink. The more DPI, the better the quality.

download   To receive information from another computer.

e-mail   Electronic mail automatically passed through computer networks and/or by modems over common-carrier lines. Beginning to be used for job-hunting letters.

facsimile   Commonly known as fax; a system used for the transmission of images of documents over telephone lines.

file   A collection of related computer information, usually organized in a directory.

font   A collection of letters and other characters used in printing type; all are the same typeface and the same size. Courier 10 point, **Courier Bold 12 point**, and *Courier Italic 10 point* are three separate fonts.

format   A command that tells the computer to create logical sectors on a disk, readying it to accept information. Or, when you format a document, such things as margins, spaces, and lengths of lines.

gigabyte   Approximately 1 billion bytes.

glitch   A problem, a malfunction.

hard disk   A storage medium that is a permanent part of the computer, stores large amounts of information, and accesses that information very rapidly.

hardware In the world of computers, anything you can touch.

integrated circuit Tiny pieces of silicon onto which electronic circuits are formed (see *chips*). Not to be confused with "silicon."

INTEL The U.S. company that developed and produced the microprocessor that makes the PC possible. The term "386" or "486" comes from Intel 80386 or 80486 equipment.

interface Computerized communication between peripheral devices—CPU to printer or CPU to mouse.

kilobyte A total of 1,024 bytes.

kiosk A stand-alone information delivery system often used for retail directories and other interactive information and sales presentations. Employment kiosks are beginning to appear; they present applicants with on-screen applications to fill out.

LAN Local area network—a hooking together of two or more computers in one location.

laser printer A printer that uses laser technology to print high-quality text and graphics. A laser-printed resume and cover letter is state-of-the-art.

letter quality A term for print characters of a quality suitable for business correspondence and similar to that of a typewriter.

Macintosh A brand name for one of Apple Computer's most popular graphics and text PCs.

megabyte Approximately 1 million bytes—known as a "meg," or referred to in print as MB.

megahertz (MHz) A measure of the speed or frequency at which the CPU operates, stated as millions of cycles per second.

memory A computer's primary storage devices—the RAM, hard-drive, ROM, internal memory.

menu A list of choices within a computer program; just what it says—dishes to be served up.

monitor The televisionlike screen allowing the user to see what the computer is doing.

mouse A pointing device used instead of a keyboard to give a computer rapid commands. Many people think it's easier to use a mouse than a keyboard.

multimedia The delivery of information that combines different media—motion video, audio, still images, graphics, animation, text.

multimedia computing Refers to the delivery of multimedia information through computers.

network A system of hardware and software allowing one computer to work together with others, usually devoted to a common job or function. (See *LAN* or *WAN*.)

OCR Optical character recognition, a software program loaded onto a PC. It works in conjunction with a scanner to read documents. OCR is how your bank uses a computer to read your checks.

offline Not currently working. A condition of being functional but not operating.

online Working great. Up and running. Electronically hooked up. A condition of being functional and operating.

operating system Software that creates the environment in which the hardware, software, and operator interact—as in "disk operating system."

peripheral device A device that attaches to the motherboard (CPU), enhancing the computer system's capabilities.

personal computer A desktop-type computer likely to be used by an individual or small business.

power users Extremely knowledgeable computer enthusiasts who eat, breathe, think, and sleep computing.

public domain A term for any material—including software programs—that can be freely copied and used with no copyright infringements.

RAM A commonly used computer term for random access memory—the working memory of the computer's system.

realtime In computing, refers to an operating mode under which data are received and immediately processed. The results are returned instantaneously. It means "right now"—not later.

ROM Read only memory—information permanently stored on microchips. It cannot be altered.

scanner An input device that digitizes information. It's the machine equivalent of human eyes.

semiconductor A term describing the electrical properties of elements such as silicon.

shareware Similar to software in public domain, shareware is written by authors who allow users to try the product before buying it. Sometimes it's free and sometimes it costs a few dollars. If the author so requests, anyone using shareware is morally obligated to send the author a contribution.

software Any set of instructions for computers. It commonly is issued on disks.

spreadsheet Computer software designed to manipulate financial or statistical information, and, by performing complex mathematical calculations, to answer "What if . . . ?" questions.

systems software Computer programs that give the computer sufficient instructions to get itself up and running and to maintain itself.

teleconference A general term for a meeting not held in person. Usually refers to a multiparty telephone call, set up by a telephone company or private source, which enables more than two callers to participate in a conversation. The growing use of video allows participants at remote locations to see, hear, and participate in proceedings, or to share visual data (video conference).

UNIX   An operating system developed by AT&T, usually found on large computers.

upload   To send information from your computer to another computer.

user   Any person who directly "uses" (operates) a computer.

user-friendly   A term used to describe aspects of computing that require only a minimum of specialized knowledge—easily understood operation and instruction, as in "Almost anyone can do this."

VDT   Video display terminal—also known as a monitor.

VGA   Video graphics array. A super VGA means a color monitor.

WAN   Wide area network—as opposed to LAN, networking that connects computers over long distances, even continent-to-continent.

Windows   The trademark name of Microsoft, Inc., for its powerful, multitask, graphical software interface for DOS-based systems.

word processing   Typing with a computer.

WYSIWYG   "What you see is what you get"—a term used to describe the good situation when a computer screen accurately shows the image of a full page of a document. Pronounced "wizzy-wig," it's a good thing for you when your resume is WYSIWYG.

Index